Fanny Wheeler Hart

Miss Hitchcock's wedding dress

Fanny Wheeler Hart

Miss Hitchcock's wedding dress

ISBN/EAN: 9783337717988

Printed in Europe, USA, Canada, Australia, Japan

Cover: Foto ©ninafisch / pixelio.de

More available books at **www.hansebooks.com**

MISS HITCHCOCK'S
WEDDING DRESS.

BY THE AUTHOR OF

"MRS. JERNINGHAM'S JOURNAL," "A VERY
YOUNG COUPLE," ETC., ETC.

THIRD THOUSAND.

NEW YORK:
SCRIBNER, ARMSTRONG & CO.
1876.

JOHN F. TROW & SON,
PRINTERS AND BOOKBINDERS,
205-213 *East 12th St.,*
NEW YORK.

CONTENTS.

CHAPTER	PAGE
I.—MIRANDA	5
II.—LADY GREGORY'S NEPHEW	22
III.—AT MADAME LA GAI'S	51
IV.—A TÊTE-À-TÊTE	75
V.—THE FIRST FLOOR	91
VI.—SUNDAY	114
VII.—FRIENDSHIP	133
VIII.—POOR MISS HITCHCOCK!	152
IX.—EXPLANATIONS	174
X.—THE CHARADE	196
XI.—LOVE	217
XII.—THE END	238

MISS HITCHCOCK'S WEDDING DRESS.

CHAPTER I.

MIRANDA.

TWO women sat together in a little room, working so hard that you could see their daily bread depended on their industry. Two women—both young, and the youngest a mere girl.

They were busy at the same piece of work—a white satin dress, covered with lace flounces, at once delicate and rich. It was made with two " bodies," one high and one low ; a white satin skirt, adorned with magnificent lace, and attached to a high bodice. Is there anyone in the world so ignorant as not to be aware that such a garment could only be intended for that most interesting of all personages —a bride ; to be worn on that most interesting of all occasions—her wedding-day ? In short, that the four hands so busily occupied were manufacturing, with light artistic touches, Somebody's wedding dress.

Both these women were lady-like in their appearance, although their clothes were shabby, and their surroundings poor and common.

The elder of the two might perhaps be thirty years old. Pale, even sallow, in coloring, with handsome dark eyes and sharply-cut features, well dressed, well fed, well tended, and happy, she might still have been called almost beautiful.

The younger, more than ten years her junior, *was* beautiful—beautiful, notwithstanding everything that conspired to make her the contrary. Tall and slight as a lily, she was also as fair as one. The delicate wild-rose tint in her cheeks was, perhaps, even more lovely than the deeper hue that might have been there but for work and confinement. Her hazel eyes were radiant, and a profusion of hair, of the same color as those eyes, covered her queen-like little head. Her features were small, delicate, and regular. She was scantily fed, she was badly dressed, she was untidy, and she was tired. Poor child! she had been steadily plying her needle for eight mortal hours ; but scantily fed, badly dressed, untidy, tired, and overworked, Miranda Maxwell was as pretty a young creature as could be seen.

" Have you nearly done, Sissy ? " said she, in her

sweet, coaxing voice, and still using the pet name, honored by old custom, which had been first given to the damsel in her teens by the little lisping baby sister. " You do look so thoroughly tired, you dear old thing. How I wish I could do all the work and let you rest."

" Rest! you foolish darling. Why should I rest more than you, I wonder?"

" Because poor old Sissy has a headache, and strong young Miranda has not one bit of ache in her whole body, and is only tired to death with working, so she knows how tired poor Sissy must be."

The elder woman smiled painfully.

" I *am* tired," she said, "and my head *does* ache —but it is of no consequence, and will pass away— and I mean to go to bed the minute I have finished, and leave you to do all the folding up and putting by. I take excellent care of myself always, you know."

" Oh, Sissy! while you are making all these smart dresses, don't you imagine the people who wear them, and the scenes they are worn in?"

" No, indeed, I don't," replied the sister, sighing.

" I do. Why, I see the white arms and neck that are to shine through these sleeves and over this lace tucker, and the slight figure that will go moving about so gracefully under all these heavy satin folds. A bride, Sissy! Just fancy how she will look," holding up the dress as she spoke; "and think of the church gay with happy people, and the pretty creature kneeling before the altar, and giving her life up to some grand fellow who adores her!"

"But, Miranda, alas! I have seen this bride, and she is so plain and so dark; she was a goose to choose white satin to be married in, and she won't look a bit nice in it."

"No, really! What a pity! And the poor grand fellow; you didn't see him too, I suppose? Does he like her, I wonder. If I was a man, I know, I couldn't fall in love with a dowdy. I should be caught by a pretty face. I am sure I should, Sissy."

"Yes; I did see him, as it happens. She brought him to Madame La Gai's, when I was in the showroom, and made him choose a bonnet for her."

"And what was he like?"

"He was handsome and tall. She seemed delighted to have him to lead about."

"Like a monkey at a fair."

"Only he was a very beautiful monkey; but he answered her quite crossly two or three times. I declare he snubbed her."

"What a shame! Fancy being snubbed by a lover."

"And he looked so handsome, and she so plain. I thought them quite an ill-matched pair; but she had a nice figure, which men think a good deal of, more than of the face sometimes. She was tall and slight like you."

"Yes. All the while I have been making the dress, I have been thinking it would just fit me. Ah, Sissy! fancy being married in such a dress as this. Wouldn't you like it?"

"My dear, doesn't it make you sorry while you work to think of all the people so much happier than you are, who wear the dresses you only make?"

"Sorry! Oh, Sissy, what a notion!"

"It would be so much wiser to try to turn your thoughts to other things. I sometimes think that there must be a purgatory for rich people, who can do what they like, and that only we poor workers shall go straight to heaven. Nothing else could make it the least fair," said the elder sister, a little bitterly.

"Why, I *like* people to be happy and everything gay, even though we can't be the same," cried Miranda, opening her lovely eyes in astonishment.

"Used you to mind the perfect happinesses of heroes and heroines, when we had time to read novels, just because they weren't yours? And making these dresses is like reading the stories of the people who wear them. Such scenes I fancy; such homes they take me into; such delightful things keep happening all the time I stitch away at pretty finery! Only black!" with a little shudder. "Oh no! I can't bear making black. I wish Madame La Gai would never sell mourning. I feel guilty, as if I was helping to make people miserable when I sew all that mournful crape on their skirts."

"Yes," said Sissy, her melancholy mouth relaxing into a smile; "you cried your eyes out over that widow's dress, till I was obliged to do it all myself, and send you out for a walk; and then we heard afterwards that Mrs. Sedgwick was a gay young creature, and did not care a bit for her cross, gouty, rather disreputable old husband—that she had married him for his money, and was rather glad than otherwise when he died."

"But how could I tell that?" cried Miranda, laughing. "I'm sure my tears were nicer than her smiles. A widow *ought* to be miserable; and, at any rate, the poor old thing had some tears shed for him, thanks to me," and she laughed again. "Only I oughtn't to have made myself unfit to help my poor Sissy—there I was as selfish as the widow herself—but I'm not so foolish now, am I, dear? I don't cry over the things, however black they may be; but they do make me sorry. And then a dress like this," again holding it up before her, for it was now completed, "makes me ready to dance for joy, when I think of the pretty, happy girl; but, oh dear! I forgot—she's ugly and cross. What a pity!"

"And now I may really go to bed," said Sissy, carefully putting up her thimble, scissors, and thread, and then indulging herself in a great stretch and thorough good yawn.

"Yes, you poor dear, you may go to bed now," replied Miranda, caressing her; "but I sha'n't come for a long time. I am going to give myself a real treat with Tennyson. Oh, how good it was of him to publish himself at last for six shillings, so that even I could get him for my own!"

"Don't sit up too late, dear."

"He's fifty times better than sleep, the magnificent creature; and weren't those nice breakfasts and dinners when I ate only just what I couldn't help, and saved up the money to buy him? I declare I was quite sorry when I'd got enough, and could eat as usual."

"Ah! my poor Miranda, when I remember all the books in papa's study!"

"Oh! don't remember, darling Sissy; please don't remember. If you begin remembering, you'll lie awake half the night; you know you will. I never remember, except to be glad that we were born ladies; and so I get comfort even from remembering—even out of our misfortunes. But you can't do that, poor dear, because you are so much wiser than I am."

"That is the folly of wisdom," replied Sissy, with one of her sad, sickly smiles.

"Now do go to bed and get a long sleep, and then you won't look so wofully tired in the morning," cried Miranda, kissing her sister, and coaxing her out of the little back parlor on the ground floor, to climb her weary way up to the garret, far above it, where they slept.

A little back parlor and a garret in a London street, with sewing and stitching from morning till night—this made the work and the life of these two women, who were born and reared in sweet country scenes, who were well educated and refined, and had once lived in ease and happiness. But they had not been the well brought-up-daughters of a much respected clergyman in vain, for they had friends still among those who had once been their father's parishioners. At his death, which had come very suddenly and in the equally unexpected wreck of his fortunes (how brought about it is not necessary to relate here as it in no way concerns this story), they might, have commanded help from their equals in rank, and been well placed in respectable families if they had chosen to support themselves as governesses. But Miranda was so young and so pretty, that Sophia, more than ten years her senior, could not bear the idea of parting with her, and sending her out into the world to try her fortunes alone. They agreed that anything was better than being separated, and so, after many consultations had been held, and many tears shed, they took to dressing the bodies of their fellow-creatures, in preference to the more "genteel" profession of adorning their minds. An old servant of their father, who was now a lodging-house keeper in a fashionable street, allowed them to live cheaply in the rooms we have described ; while Madame La Gai, a West End dressmaker, gladly supplied them with work in their own home, and occasionally employed the elder sister in the showroom. In her young and less prosperous unmarried days, she had contracted a debt of gratitude to Mr. Maxwell, for timely assistance, which she never forgot, but paid it cheerfully and with interest to his daughters.

All dressmakers are not slave-drivers; all landladies are not termagants, though modern novels generally represent them as such. The sisters met with kindness and consideration; and while Sophy mourned much for the past, the light-hearted Miranda enjoyed much in the present.

Her sister's conversation to-night, however, had tinged her thoughts with melancholy; and as she stood alone in the little chamber, with the satin dress lying on the table, it looked to her, with its lovely shining white surface, like the ghost of a dead joy, which she had never clasped in life, and which could now never be hers. She touched it timidly, and then passed her little hands down the folds of the common mouseline-de-laine frock she wore herself.

"And I, too, am so young," she said, softly, "and so gay;" and her eyes filled with tears (were they unreasonable?) as the thought of her own gayety appealed to her with an indescribable pathos.

Again she touched the two dresses with her rosy fingers, and then held up the satin robe at arm's length from her, and smiled and nodded to it as if it had been another girl.

"It is just my height," she cried; "and Sissy said her figure was like mine. Oh! only fancy me in such a dress as that!"

"Why not?" something within her cried out imperiously—"why not? Put it on; why should you not put it on?"

She laughed and blushed, and said, "What an idea!" But the something was urgent and persevering, and kept on saying, "Put it on; you will like it; it is such an innocent pleasure, and so new. With all the dresses you have made, you never thought of this before; put it on!"

She slipped off her common well-worn frock, and stood in her petticoat, with bare white arms and neck. Then, rather breathlessly, she put on the muslin skirt worn under the robe, and then the dress itself, fastening it carefully, and shaking out the folds and flowers with light, joyful fingers.

It fitted her exactly.

"But oh!" she cried, "I must see her." She spoke of herself in that bridal finery as if she was somebody else. "I can't see her; I should like to see her!"

There was no mirror in the dingy back parlor, but she knew that in the front room there was a large one, and she also knew that the inhabitants of that room had gone out for the evening.

With a little laugh, and clapping her hands for a quick hasty minute, she ran into the adjoining apartment, and danced forward to the looking-glass, where, with quite a start of delight and astonishment, she beheld the radiant creature she had come to see.

"How pretty she is! how dear she is! Oh, you beautiful darling!" and the glowing lips met the other lips in the mirror with a sweet girl-kiss. "But you know, my dear, you must do your hair properly, like the ladies you see."

In those days it was easy to dress such hair as hers, hanging, as it did, in rich, but rather short natural curls all over her head. It had only to be frizzed about and disordered a little, and raised over combs in imitation of puffs, and it made, in its bright, golden-brown tangle, a very fashionable coiffure.

A pair of white kid gloves lay on the table; apparently they had been tried on by one of the occupants of the room, and, not fitting, had been thrown down in haste. Miranda, having finished dressing her hair took them up.

"Six and a-half," she said, "your very number;" and she held them in her hand, and curtsied to the girl in the looking-glass, to whom she showed them; "your very number, you know. But you must not put them on, or you will be found out, you naughty little thief;" and she shook her fist at the laughing, radiant creature she kept curtseying to all the time she spoke. "You laugh, do you? fie, fie! Why you ought to be ashamed of yourself; you know you ought."

And then she began to dance.

Presently she stole softly up stairs into Sissy's room, where that poor weary woman lay breathing deeply, in the heavy sleep of the overworked. How sallow, worn, and old her face looked on the shabby pillow! But Miranda, dearly as she loved it, was too well accustomed to that tired face to have any new sorrow aroused by it; though, to my mind, a worn soul in a sleeping face is the saddest of all the sad sights which this mysterious world can show us.

On tiptoe, with her finger on her lips, she approached a chest of drawers, and unlocked one of them which she knew contained some treasures—a few things, a few luxuries belonging to the prosperous past. Things—some of them kept almost accidentally, and because it had not been known what else to do with them than to keep them; and others because it would have been too painful to part with them, on account of associations connected with their givers, or with happy moments in which they were given. She turned them all over noiselessly, and quite triumphantly held up a pair of white satin boots and a little red opera cloak. Then she opened the morocco case in which lay the family jewels, that had sometimes, in her childish days, been displayed to her wondering, admiring eyes, and took out the dear old grandmother's pins—two diamond stars for the hair—and her black velvet ribbon for the neck, clasped with glittering diamonds. Hastily she adorned head, neck, shoulders, and feet with all this pretty finery, and, pausing at the foot of the bed, longed to wake up Sophy, that she might have the pleasure of seeing her so brilliant and so fair. " She has not an idea how nice I am," she thought ; " but I must not wake her, poor Sissy. She might lie too long awake if I did." Then she ran rapidly down stairs to the front sitting room. " If Sissy mustn't see me, I may see myself," she cried, as she stood before the mirror.

The diamonds sparkled in her hair, and her eyes sparkled beneath the diamonds.

"How lovely girls are when they are dressed!" she said, almost regretfully; "and such a fright as I am in my stuff frock! Who would have thought it?"

At this moment a noise of many carriages, that appeared all just to pass the house and then to stop abruptly, drew her attention to the window, and, peeping through the shutters, she saw, in the broad moonlight of the summer night, vehicle after vehicle drive up to the door of the next house, and there deposit their freight of richly-attired women and black-coated men, who instantly disappeared through it; while suddenly, from within it, a burst of dance music made a joyful sound, like an invitation to be happy. "And I am dressed like them; I look like them. I might run in among them—dance, laugh, talk, and be happy too!" she cried. Then, with a look of astonishment—"Why shouldn't I?" and she burst into a fit of soft laughter, and for a moment danced up and down on the same spot, like a delighted child.

Then, in an instant, without waiting to reflect (had she so waited, this story would never have been written), she slipped out of the house, and, running a few steps on the pavement, entered the one next door. Some ladies who had just descended from their carriage preceded her, and she followed them as closely as if she belonged to their party. Two richly-dressed elderly women and three young ones, in floating draperies of blue and white, were the pioneers in whose steps Miranda trod. When they gave their cloaks to the attending servants, she did the same with hers ; and when they declined tea, she also passed on with only a bow of her head; and so they walked up the crowded staircase towards the ballroom, still followed by this happy, innocent, daring, imprudent creature, who felt at the same moment as if she was in a dream, and yet as if she had never been so vividly awake in all her life before.

At the head of the staircase, just within the threshold of the drawing-room, stood a stately woman, magnificently attired, who bowed and smiled to all the guests, and occasionally shook hands with a favored few as they entered ; and Miranda and her five ladies, in due turns came in for their share of these salutations. There was a crowd in the room, but a crowd still pressing onward to something beyond; and Miranda, as she looked about her in painful bewilderment, observed that the younger ladies were all sooner or later accosted by gentlemen, and led off into a large inner apartment, where a waltz was being danced. Suddenly she, too, was addressed. A tall, very good-looking man, who had been watching her for some moments, though she was not in the least aware that he had been doing so, offered her his arm, saying, "May I have the pleasure?" and she found herself in the next room before she knew where she was.

CHAPTER II.

LADY GREGORY'S NEPHEW.

"YOU will excuse my not waiting for an introduction," said he, immediately; "but I am Lady Gregory's nephew."

Miranda laughed gayly, and, being quite ignorant of the force of the argument contained in those words, replied simply, "Are you really?"

"Yes; so, though I have not had the pleasure of meeting you before, I thought I might venture."

She laughed again.

"Oh! is it not beautiful?" she cried, softly—"the flowers, the music. Do you always live like this?"

"Yes, always," replied he, not understanding the situation.

"How happy you must be!" sighed Miranda. "How different lives are—and all the girls are pretty!" she added, looking round her with delight.

"It is not in that you find the difference," he replied, with smiling gallantry.

She turned her lovely eyes frankly upon him.

"It is in everything," she said ; "but, ah ! you don't understand ; how should you ?"

"I think I do, though," answered he, with a sort of eagerness, and looking at her very kindly, as he first discovered with what earnestness her remarks were made. "I think I do understand. This is your first ball ; is not that it ? "

"*That* it ! " she cried, almost in scorn. "Well, it is my first ball. I never was at one before."

"Yes," he said, watching the play of her countenance with an interest to which he was quite unaccustomed ; "so I see ; and I think also that it is your first visit to London. You come from some delightful country home—a parsonage, perhaps," but here his eye, as it scanned her, fell on the diamonds, the rich satin and expensive lace ; "no, not that, but some bright, flower-covered dwelling, and you are new to town and town gaieties."

Miranda gave her hands a little joyful clap, and laughed gleefully, like a child.

"Oh, you wizard ! " she said ; "do you think that ? " No heart could resist such a sweet, gay laugh, and her partner laughed too, and looked almost affectionately down into her transparent eyes.

"Yes," he said, boldly, "I do. I will venture to pronounce that you are not a London young lady."

"Ah!" she cried; "and what else?"

"What else?" replied he, smiling. "I think, then, that you are always quite happy; not only in a gay scene like this, but in your own pretty home also."

"Are you a fortune-teller?" asked she, shaking her fair head, crowned with its rich tangle of bright hair and diamond stars.

"A fortune-teller? Not for the future, I am afraid, though I may guess a little about the past and present."

"I wish you were. I wish you could tell my future," said Miranda, turning her sweet, innocent face towards him as she spoke.

"I wish I could," he cried, with a sudden eagerness quite unexpected to himself, and looking at her as, perhaps, in all his thirty years of life, he had never yet looked at a woman; then, cooling down, even more surprised at his own feelings than at the fresh simplicity that had excited them, he added, "but I am, as I said, for the past and for the present; and being so, I recognize your life as an exceptionally happy one. I think you are always happy."

"I am always happy, am I?" she said; and nodded

her head with a little knowing air that was perfectly enchanting. "Yes, so I am; and my life is an exceptionally happy one? No indeed! *that* it isn't. It is exceptionally the other way; and I am happy in spite of my life."

Then, to his dismay, he found that the beautiful eyes were filling with tears, while one crystal drop overflowed and hung on the long lashes for an instant, ere the little hand brushed it away.

He, too, felt ready to cry, and said to himself, indignantly, " So this is the result of your stupid ballroom talk, when it strikes against a true, earnest nature."

"My dear child," he said aloud, in quite a paternal manner, "I beg your pardon. I didn't mean; please don't mind; but—" and he added this question because he really could not help it, he felt so sorry, "*are* not you happy?"

"Yes, I am," she answered frankly. "But then it's *I* that am happy, not my life."

"I am so sorry," he said, with hearty sincerity and a sort of penitent air, as if he felt himself to blame in the matter.

She smiled. "But you needn't mind," she said; "I don't."

Then there was a little pause between them, while

the lovely eyes watched the dancers wistfully, and were afterwards raised to his with quite a pathetic expression of entreaty.

"*Might* I dance?" she asked. "I do so wish it."

He looked at her with mingled amusement and delight. He confessed to himself that he had never before been so captivated by any girl, or had ever before met with any girl in the least like her. Her freshness alone was sufficient to enchant him; and when to such freshness of character was added such fresh beauty of face, he felt as if he had suddenly become a believer in the possibility, at least, of love at first sight. He would certainly have preferred to continue talking to her, but no man could resist her pathetic "*Might* I dance?" And as, next to her conversation, to dance with her was the greatest pleasure he could at the moment imagine, he very willingly began to waltz.

For a few steps it seemed doubtful whether their styles suited, or, indeed, whether Miranda had any style at all; but either she soon remembered what she had once learned, or she acquired knowledge with surprising rapidity, for after those few steps, her dancing, even to his fastidious taste, was as charming as herself.

I hardly know which of the two enjoyed the waltz most; and when it was over, he did not feel in the least inclined to leave her side, but walked her round and round the room as often as etiquette permitted.

"Oh!" she cried, suddenly putting her hand up to her eyes, as if something hurt them. "Who is that poor woman who is scowling so? Can it be with me she is so angry? or is she like a picture, and seems to look at everybody who looks at her?"

"Who do you mean? Where? I don't see."

"There, that poor woman in blue, who is so—so ugly—and so brown—so very brown—an Indian, perhaps. You must see her now under those lights, and scowling at me—at least she seems as if she was."

"Oh yes! I see her now."

"And who is she?"

"She is—a Miss Hitchcock," replied he, with extraordinary bitterness in his voice and face.

"Miss Hitchcock! Oh! you don't really mean it."

"Why not?"

"Oh, how very, very odd! And is that really Miss Hitchcock! Yes, to be sure; she is just like what Sissy said. And now, where is Mr. Cressingham, poor man? I'm sorry for him; he ought to be with her; but he can't be that man she's dancing with, I know."

"Can't he? Why not?"

"Oh! that man is short and insignificant, and Mr. Cressingham is *extremely* good-looking and tall and nice."

"Is he?" replied her partner, laughing. "Do you know him, then?"

"No, I don't know him; but I have heard him described. Point him out to me, please."

He looked first at her, and then all about the room, and then at her again; after which he said, slowly, "Do you know, it's very odd, but I don't see him anywhere."

"He ought to be with her," she replied, gravely.

"Ought he? but why?".

"Oh! because—" she began quickly, and added in a lower voice, "they are engaged to be married."

"And must people who are engaged to be married always go in couples, poor things?"

"Poor things?" cried she indignantly. "What! if they care for each other?" but she paused in the middle of the speech, and said the last words a little shyly, when she found what they were going to be.

"In *some* cases, yes, of course," he answered, catching light from her eyes, and seeming for the moment capable of feeling anything himself.

"In *some* cases," repeated Miranda, looking greatly astonished. Then she reflected a little, and added, "Well, I suppose that is true, and that this is not one of them ; for I have heard that she is very cross—oh! doesn't she look so?—and *snubs* him."

"Snubs him!" cried her partner, frowning. "Oh! they say that, do they?"

"Yes, indeed ; and they say worse things than that. Do you know, he can't be really nice, though he *is* so handsome"—here she spoke quite confidentially—" for I do almost believe he is marrying her for her money."

"How shocking!" replied he. His voice sounded bitter and sarcastic, and he colored so much as he spoke, that she saw he was quite as indignant at the idea of a mercenary marriage as she was herself.

"Yes, isn't it?" she said, simply. "Only fancy what their lives will be when they are married."

"No, don't fancy it," he answered, quickly. "Perhaps they never will be married."

"Oh yes!" cried she, opening her eyes wide; "they will. Why, the wedding day is fixed and the dress *made;*" and she glanced down at her satin robe and laughed a little.

"And yet the marriage may not take place," persisted he. "I have known marriages broken off—yes, at the very altar."

Miranda opened her lovely brown eyes even wider than she had opened them before, as if she was taking in new and alarming ideas. "But that is *very* wrong," she said, slowly, with a great emphasis on the very.

"Is it?" cried he, with eagerness. "Are you sure?"

"Yes, I suppose so. I am. Am I not? Can there be any doubt?"

"It seems to me there can. Now look here; which is worst—to break a promise, or to swear a lie?"

"To break a promise, or to swear a lie?" repeated Miranda, absolutely appalled; "but both are impossible—nobody could do either."

"Oh! couldn't they?" cried he, bitterly; "and does nobody ever make a mistake, then? Why, what a delightful world this is we are living in!"

"A mistake?"

"Yes, a mistake; there *are* such things as mistakes, I do assure you. Suppose, now, that two people are engaged to be married, and one of them finds out that he (or shall we say she?) does not really care for the other, shall he (or she) break the first promise—there's a broken promise, you see—or shall he (or she) go to the church and there perjure himself (and there's the sworn lie), and so begin a life of deceit that never ends?"

Her innocent face clouded over, as a child's, or perhaps an angel's, might, who hears of sin for the first time.

"Yes," she said, slowly and sadly, "that might happen; I suppose it might. But it is *too* painful, isn't it? Why should we imagine such things?"

"Let us just for one little minute," persisted he, pleadingly, "while you tell me what that unhappy person ought to do."

"How can I tell?" said she, simply; "but there can't be any doubt, can there?"

"Well," he cried, with great eagerness, "what should he do, then?"

"Tell her the truth, of course, and ask her to release him."

"And if she refuses?"

"But she couldn't refuse."

"Couldn't she? Well, please—just for the sake of the argument, you know—suppose she *did?*"

"Then, of course, he must marry her."

She spoke as if she announced an undoubted fact, and he listened to the words as if they were an oracle.

"What!" he cried, and a sudden pain came into his face; "do you really think so?"

"Yes, certainly; there can't be two opinions on the subject; don't you think so too?"

"And swear false vows—swear to love and honor, when he does neither?"

"No, no!" she cried, distressed and eager; "he would have told her, and he would try to do his very best; there would be no falseness in it; and he would be helped; he would pray—" she stopped suddenly, blushing crimson, and something like a tear glistened on her eyelashes. "Oh!" she cried, "*don't* talk of such things here; it is irreverent."

"Divine innocence!" exclaimed he, with enthusiasm.

But she did not hear the words, neither did she observe the look of tender admiration with which he was regarding her. She was too busy controlling her own feelings to trouble herself about his.

"She would be such a *horrid* woman, who would make him, after he had told her, you know," she said at last.

"Yes; but there *are* horrid women, in the world."

"I suppose there are," said she, reluctantly. "*Isn't* it a pity?"

"Yes, it is a pity, when one thinks of the misery they cause. You are only thinking of her; but do, please, think of *him* for a minute. Is he to be miserable for ever, only just because he has made a mistake?" He spoke quite impatiently.

"Only just?" cried she, shaking her head, "Oh! but it is a great deal more than that. There must be something very wrong, indeed, about him, before he could make that sort of a mistake, you know;" and the little head nodded very decidedly and emphatically here. "A *good* man wouldn't do it."

"A *good* man," repeated he, discontentedly; "but so few men *are* good."

Her eyes turned upon him, radiant with surprise and a sort of indignation.

"So few men good!" she cried, "What an idea! How little you know!"

Another waltz was playing now.

"They are dancing again," she said, "and it is so delicious! Please, I don't understand—what happens—do we change partners, or—*how* do we manage?"

"Where is her chaperone?" thought the gentleman. "Surely she came in with Mrs. Nesbit. How can she be so completely left to herself?"

"No," he answered, basely; "we don't change partners; we go on dancing together as long as we like."

"Then *shall* we begin again? It is such waste of time, when we *might* be dancing! It seems almost wrong; don't you think so?"

"Decidedly," answered he; and they commenced waltzing.

When next they stopped, she instantly spoke breathlessly, with a little joyful laugh.

"Can the lives in the different planets," she asked, "be more different than the different lives in this one?"

Three "differents" in one sentence; but he only added three more to them in the reply which his lips uttered, while his eyes were bent in keen admiration on her sweet, animated face.

"And can the girls in different planets be more

different," he said, "than the different girls in this one?"

A surprised look in her face, as if thoughts racing rapidly to an end had been brought to a sudden check before they reached it. She glanced round her.

"Are they?" she said, doubtfully; "but no"— and again came that joyous child's laugh—"girls *are* so like, only you don't know it; how should you? It's different dresses does it all."

"As now?" asked he, puzzled.

"Ah!" she cried, nodding her pretty head confidentially, "*don't* I look like them all now? And if you could see me at home! Why, I had not the least idea what I was like."

He caught her meaning.

"This is your first appearance in such splendid plumage, I daresay," he answered, smilingly; "but still, at home, I don't suppose you are quite a Cinderella."

"Yes, I am!" cried she, delighted; "that is just what I am! Dear Cinderella! don't you love the story? or didn't you when you were a child? I always *was* so fond of it, and how little I thought" —She burst out laughing, and, in her light-hearted glee, seemed almost dancing where she stood.

"And the wicked sisters," said he. "Do you carry out the story into all its particulars?"

"No, indeed. Poor old Sissy! What a shame! And yet—yes—partly, even in *that;* for she *would* be surprised if she knew I was here."

"And the slipper," he continued, very much amused—"the slipper. I hope you will leave me the slipper. I am the Prince, of course."

"As to that," she cried, "see!" and, raising her dress a little half-inch, her foot peeped out.

"Boots!" he cried; "but never mind. The foot that wears them is small enough to be Cinderella's own. How I should like to find you some morning among your cinders. May I come and try?"

"Oh yes, certainly; you may come and try."

"When next I call on Mrs. Nesbit, I shall go down the area steps into the kitchen."

"Will you? That will be very humble of you. But what in the world will you do it for?"

"Why, in order to find Cinderella among her cinders!"

"Oh! I see—yes—Mrs. Nesbit," speaking slowly and looking about her, till her eye fell on the lady in whose train she had entered the room. "Yes, of course."

Then they danced again.

"Do you know Miss Hitchcock?" she asked, as the waltz stopped playing.

He started more perceptibly than at all became a man of the world, but answered immediately, "Yes, I do a little."

"She looks horrid. Is she?"

"Yes, very horrid."

"Poor thing! how trying it must be!"

"What?" asked he, frowning.

"Why, to be like that! Fancy being that one's self. I do pity her; don't you?"

"Not a bit; I pity those who have to do with her, not her."

"How odd it all is! how little I thought I should meet her to-night! I wonder what she thinks of *me;* she *does* keep looking at me, doesn't she?" then, suddenly frightened, "Oh! is it me or my dress she's looking at?"

"I'm sure I don't know; why, at you, of course, not at your dress. What should she look at your dress for? Its charmingly pretty—white and shiny and all that; but it's nothing remarkable, is it? But why do you keep on thinking so much about Miss Hitchcock at all? Verily, it's doing her too much honor."

"Ah! but there's a reason I can't tell you why I can't help thinking about her—there is indeed."

A gentleman who had been for some time looking a great deal at Miranda, now approached her, and asked her partner to introduce him. He made the necessary senseless signs, and uttered the accustomed unintelligible sounds, and the ceremony of introduction was complete.

The gentleman immediately asked her to dance with him, but she smiled, and replied that she could not, as she was dancing with—and here she paused, and glanced towards her partner for help, as she did not know his name.

He did not return her glance for some reason or other—he was looking down on the floor.

"Yes, but that waltz is over; may I not hope for the next?" persisted the stranger.

"But I am going on dancing with him," she replied, with the greatest simplicity.

"Oh, indeed!" was the answer, while the gentleman looked with surprise, first at the one and then at the other.

Miranda's face was cool and bright; while Lady Gregory's nephew never lifted his eyes from the floor, bit his lip, and uttered not a word. After a moment's hesitation, the new-comer bowed gravely and retired. He went straight across the room and entered into conversation with Miss Hitchcock, their eyes being pointedly directed, while they talked, towards Miranda and her partner.

"What did he mean?" asked Miranda; but she received no answer.

"That poor thing keeps looking at me like an evil eye, and makes me quite nervous," continued she, with a little shiver.

"Come into the next room," he said; "the music has stopped, the dance is over for the present, and there we can take a turn safe from the persecution of an eye that I must own, is an evil one."

"Don't you pity ugly people?" said Miranda. "It's no wonder they're cross; it *must* be trying."

"I don't mind it a bit."

She looked at him, astonished, and then began to laugh.

"Oh! but you are not—" she cried, and then stopped, blushing and laughing again. "How absurd you are! I won't say it, because you said it on purpose to make me."

"Say what?"

"Oh you—oh now—oh no!—nothing at all."

"And yet you won't say it, because I said it to make you say it. How very obliging! Thank you very much."

"There is nothing to thank me for."

"Isn't there? Well now, do you know, I thought I had a great deal to thank you for; but, seriously, and to return to the question you put to me, I don't think it matters one bit to people themselves, their being ugly. It is their neighbors who suffer."

"Do you think so? I don't. Perhaps men don't care, but girls must. Now that poor Miss Hitchcock; just fancy being as ugly as she is. I do pity her."

"I pity her husband more."

"Her husband? Oh no; I don't pity *him* in the least; he needn't be her husband, but she must be herself. He has chosen her out of all the world. Why should you pity him?"

"Because I think he is a most consummate ass."

"With all my heart; but we needn't pity him for that."

"I beg your pardon. An indifferently sensible man, who behaves like an ass, is one of the most pitiable people in the world."

"And is he indifferently sensible?"

"He is generally accounted so; he is supposed to have ordinary abilities."

"Oh well! you know what I think of him. He is making a mercenary marriage. One can't but despise him; and the cleverer he is, the worse he is."

"You are a severe judge."

"We must be—mustn't we?—of what is paltry and mean, or we shouldn't keep high-minded ourselves, should we?"

"Paltry and mean!" repeated he.

She was surprised at his manner.

"Why do you repeat my words?" she said.

"Oh! nothing," he replied, very quietly; "only I believe Mr. Cressingham is not generally considered paltry and mean. I never happened to hear the words applied to him before, that is all."

"Well, perhaps I oughtn't to have said it, but it will do him no harm my applying them; it is a small matter what I think of him."

"Won't it? is it?" answered he.

"The world is wide, these things are small;
If they are nothing, what is there at all?"

"Oh!" said she, smiling, "you are a reader of Monkton Milnes."

"Are those lines from Monkton Milnes?"

"Did not you know it? He writes charming poetry, and never gets the credit of anything."

"Oh! but I think he does; he has a very high reputation," replied her partner.

"I don't know. You see you quoted him without knowing it; and then I always think it *is* such a shame that Tennyson gets all the credit of the grand couplet about 'lov'd and lost,' when poor Monkton Milnes said it first."

"'Twere better to have lov'd and lost
Than never to have lov'd at all,'"

quoted her partner, in musical accents; "but what do you mean? Surely nobody said *that* before Tennyson? surely not Monkton Milnes? When and where?"

She repeated softly, and without too much expression for a ballroom—

"'He who for love has undergone
The worst that can befall,
Is happier, thousand-fold, than one
Who never lov'd at all.

A grace within his soul hath reigned,
Which nothing else can bring;
Thank God for all that I have gained
By this high suffering.'"

"Beautiful verses!" cried he; "and are those

Lord Houghton's? Then, after all, Tennyson only condensed what Milnes said before him!"

"Yes, really, that was all; and I have some notion that the idea comes originally from a Spanish poet," added she.

"And I have little doubt that, like almost everything else, some Latin fellow said it first of all."

"No, really; and *isn't* it curious that Tennyson should have got all the credit?"

"You are not an admirer of Tennyson."

"*I* not an admirer of Tennyson?" and her cheeks flushed a lovely pink, while her eyes grew more radiant than ever. "Why, I have him of my own, and I saved up to buy him. I—ah! you don't know—you couldn't guess—not if you tried forever—what I did in order to get Tennyson; and I declare," she cried, with sudden remorse, "I meant to have been reading him all this evening, and here I am instead!"

She looked really quite distressed, and he hastened to comfort her.

"Well," he said, smiling, "you are talking of him and quoting him, if you are not reading him; and that is almost as good, I suppose."

It was a hot summer night, and while thus conversing, they had stepped out into a balcony full of flowers, that hung over the street. The ballrooms looked gay and fairy-like, seen under the festooned arch of bright-tinted drapery, like a new world of radiant lights and lovely colors—apart, yet so near —of which they did not form a portion; and yet, viewing it as they did, from the cool, calm outer world, where they stood alone, which appeared as if it had been created only that they might so view it. They stood leaning their backs against the railing of the balcony, looking into the ballroom, when, suddenly, the dwellers therein began to pass in couples across the room, all going in the same direction, and there disappearing and not returning again.

"Where are they going?" asked Miranda.

"To supper," replied Lady Gregory's nephew; and he offered her his arm, and prepared to re-enter the room.

As he did so, the window in the next house—that house where Miranda lived, and which also looked into a balcony, divided from the one in which they stood by only a low railing—was thrown open by some one in the room inside. A bright idea at the same moment struck Miranda—an idea which she accepted with regret, and yet which she felt must be acted on. At intervals during that splendidly happy evening, a vague uneasiness had filled her mind as to how she could return. It had been easy to get *there*, but how—how—how—*how* could she return back again? How, even if she managed to escape, could she stand alone on the door-steps of her own house in the late night or early morning hours, and ring the bell and knock? If a servant was roused by the sounds she made, or her landlady herself, how could she explain what she had been doing, to account for her being alone at that hour on the door-steps in Miss Hitchcock's wedding dress? And if no one was roused, there would be policemen, and possibly, passers-by, to stare at her and wonder who she was, and, perhaps, even to stop and ask her questions.

Now a means of escape seemed offered to her as unexpected as it was easy. She was aware that a gentleman had taken the drawing-room floor only that day. He had probably spent the evening out, and on his late return had opened the window. It was as if it had been all done only for her.

She looked at her partner, her eyes full of regret. Oh! how happy she was, and how she liked him! Never had she conversed in this way with anyone before; never had she liked anyone half so much. Of course she should never see him again—never speak to him again. Of course he would not give her another thought; but she should remember him all her life—he would have a niche in her heart entirely his own; and when she was an old woman, she knew she should still think with delight of this wonderful evening, and of the man who had danced with her on it—"Yes, I am sure I shall," she said to herself, "unless I am a very ungrateful old woman."

Just reflect for one moment what her life was, and what this evening must have been to her.

She did not take his arm, and she looked at him *very* sorrowfully.

"It is too warm for supper. I could not eat anything," she said. "If you would bring me a glass of lemonade here, would you? I should be so much obliged."

He was gone directly.

"Oh! why was he in such a hurry? Alas!" she sighed "he is gone, and I shall never see him again." She felt so much more moved than she had expected to do, or could at all understand, that she stood for the moment like one bewildered. "Oh! I should like to run after him," she said to herself, "just for one minute. Why did I not thank him for having made me so happy? How heartless I was! and I shall never see him again." And then she found that she had been crying.

So she thought it was time to act, and after looking about her as if she was afraid of being seen (as indeed she was), she softly and nimbly climbed over the railing that divided the two balconies, and stood in the one that belonged to the drawing-room of her own house. The window, as we said before, was wide open. A light streamed through it, which seemed dim enough to Miranda's eyes, still sparkling, as it were, from the brilliant illuminations in the ballroom. Probably it was a single candle, lighted by the new lodger on his return home. Happy man! he had a latch-key, and so could let himself in at any hour he pleased, and no one who saw him at any hour of the night, standing on the doorsteps and opening the door with it, would feel the faintest emotion even of a surprise, and this only just because he was a man and not a woman. Miranda was not at all inclined to stand up for the rights of women; but it *did* occur to her at that moment, as a great injustice, that only men should be allowed a latch-key.

And now, where was the lodger, and what was he

doing? If she could only know whether he had his back to the window or not. If he had, she might glide in, and pass so noiselessly and gently across the room, that he would not know she was there till she was gone.

Time was precious. It was no use hesitating; she must act at once, and bear the consequences, whatever they might be.

And so she crossed the threshold of the open French window and entered the room.

A single candle burned on the table in the centre. A man was standing—yes, actually with his back to the window, stooping over another small table in the corner just opposite the door.

Miranda glided forward like a ghost, but as she did so—was it mere accident? or was it that mysterious consciousness of an existence beyond our own approaching us, which we have all of us, I suppose, felt in one way or other (the most frequent way, perhaps, being that the gaze of a pair of eyes directed towards the sleeping face will recall the soul from the land of dreams, and bring it back, startled and half reluctant, to this work-a-day world)?—whatever was the cause, whether commonplace or metaphysical, the new lodger, as Miranda entered the room, began slowly raising himself from his stooping posture and preparing to turn round.

She perceived the danger, and, quick as thought, blew out the candle. "Hullo!" cried an astonished, voice; and then, as she made her way rapidly towards the door, a match was suddenly struck, and the little blaze of light directed full towards her retreating figure. But she was gone; breathlessly she flew up the stairs. Alas! the gas still burned on the staircase. She felt rather than heard she was pursued; but the door was yet between them, and she had a minute's start of her pursuer. She knew—and he, of course, did not—of a housemaid's cupboard full of brooms and brushes at the head of the first flight of stairs, the door of which was papered over and scarcely visible; and before the drawing-room door opened, and the amazed new lodger made his appearance on the staircase, Miranda—satin dress, lace flounces, diamonds and all—was safely ensconced in this closet, among Nancy's implements for making everything clean and tidy but themselves.

She heard him walking about with heavy steps in a vague, changeable way: first he was running, then he stopped, then seemed to be taking little turns in different directions, and, as she thought softly opening doors and peeping inside them, and every now and then she heard him say, " By Jove !"

Poor Miranda! she laughed to that degree that she could hardly stand; she laughed till she cried, and till the suppression of all sound, and the violent effort by which that suppression was attained, became actual pain. At last, however, and a very long at last it seemed to the imprisoned girl, she heard the unfortunate new lodger return to his room ; and then, after a delay of a few moments, from the fear that he might make another raid, she liberated herself from her uncomfortable and cramped position, and fled noiselessly up stairs to her garret.

There lay Sophy in heavy, undisturbed sleep; and there Miranda divested herself of all her lovely borrowed plumes. She looked around on the shabby garret she knew so well, with its sloping roof, rickety furniture, and carpetless floor, and crept into the bed where, night after night, she had lain so sleepily down by Sophy's side, and she wondered whether she was indeed the same girl who had been waltzing in the brilliant ballroom with Lady Gregory's nephew, or whether she should not, on waking the following morning, find that it was all a dream.

CHAPTER III.

AT MADAME LA GAI'S.

THE next morning Sophy was ill. Poor, patient, hard-working Sophy! She lifted her head from her pillow to find it all light and giddy; and when she tried to get up, she fainted away. Her fainting roused Miranda, wrapped in the soundest, sweetest sleep by her side. She rose hastily to attend on her sister, and had replaced her in bed, restored her fluttering senses, rapidly dressed herself, and made poor Sophy some hot tea, before —her eye happening to fall on the satin dress hanging on the door—the wonderful events of the preceding evening flashed on her mind. Up to that moment she had forgotten them as entirely as if they had never happened; and when they came back to her memory, they came all at once with a sudden rush, and she recognized them as a part of her life which had somehow wrought a change; if not, alas! in that life, at least in her who led it.

First of all, as she looked at the dress, she gave a great start, and a crimson blush spread all over her beautiful face; then she laughed—a little, chuckling, child-like laugh—and then tears came into her sweet eyes and hung on their long dark lashes.

"Poor Sissy!" she said; "poor, *poor* Sissy! so ill, and with nothing pleasant to think of!"

She kissed her vehemently. Sophy opened her tired eyes, and saw lovely Miranda standing there kissing her, as brilliant as a morning in the depth of June, her lips still smiling, and the bright color in her cheeks seeming all the pinker for the tears glittering on it.

"Why do you do that?" she said in her weary voice, faint and hoarse now from illness.

"I love you so, Sissy," said Miranda. "I am so sorry for you. I wish you had been at a ball last night."

Sophie stared at her.

"Wish *what?*" she said.

"Oh, that you had something pleasant to think of!" cried Miranda, impatiently. "All the pleasures in your life have become pains when you remember them. They are pains now, just because they were pleasures then; and that is so *hard* upon you, that I can hardly bear it."

"It won't matter when I am dead," replied Sophy, so quietly, and with such a wild look in her eyes, that the contrast between her voice and her eyes was quite horrible.

Miranda gave a little scream, and rushed down stairs to call Mrs. Green, their friendly landlady, to her sister.

"Dear heart!" said that good woman, when she had examined the patient, "the poor thing's just worn out like, and no wonder, it's that weary stitching and stitching, and no pleasure at all; and she's feverish; it's rest she wants, Miss Miranda, and then, when she's better, a blow of country air on her white cheeks to make her strong again. Poor lady! she's too *quiet* under her troubles; and so she goes on and on, and nobody knowin', till a day comes when she breaks down all at onct."

By this time Sophy had sunk into a heavy sleep, and Miranda began, slowly and sorrowfully, to put the finery in which she had been so happy the night before carefully away.

Afterwards she sat in the little parlor below

making a black silk mantle, which was part of Miss Hitchcock's trousseau.

What a life it was for a young girl to lead—born a gentlewoman, bred among green fields, sweet English gardens, and furze-scented commons—to sit there working all day long in a dingy room looking into a dingier court, the only creature belonging to her lying ill in bed worn out with hardships, and she conscious that if she ceased working they might both starve!

And yet, while she sat there busily plying her needle, she sang.

First she just warbled little snatches of melody, that floated round her for a moment, as the bright young voice sent them forth into the world, and then disappeared—somehow and somewhere—but how and where? Did they cease to exist, dying almost at their birth? or do they still live? and do *all* sweet sounds once uttered live on through all ages and give pleasure for ever?

Then after a time she sang the following song:—

> " I will rob the linnet
> On his leafy throne
> Of the sweetest minute
> He has ever known.

"Listen to his chanting,
  Undismayed by art;
Nothing *can* be wanting
  In a linnet's heart.

"All my life hath given—
  All the joys that live—
Ev'rything but Heaven
  I will gladly give,

"Just to be one minute,
  Ere my life is done,
Happy as a linnet
  Singing to the sun."

Then she began to laugh. "Such nonsense!" she said; "as if a linnet was happier than a girl! Why, it can't dance! I can sing, and I can dance, too, and it can only sing. Why, if I was in a tree, and my face turned up to the sweet blue sky, and I singing, I would defy any linnet to be one bit happier than I should be there; and after that I could dance, and a poor little linnet could only fly; and I fly in my dreams. I have often flown when I'm asleep, and its not to *compare* with dancing. Do birds dream, I wonder? and do they dance in their dreams? That would make a difference, I admit. But the happiest dreams are not so happy as happiness! Happiness is such a *delicious* thing; there is nothing like it—nothing! It always seems to me as if we were made for happiness, and all the rest was a mistake. Just like fine weather—beautiful, fine weather is the *real* thing, and the rain is just a mistake; but not clouds—they are so *lovely!* Clouds are sometimes the loveliest thing on earth, only they are not on earth; they are in the sky, and perhaps that is why they are more beautiful than anything else. They are *near* heaven, and that may be why happiness is so beautiful; for in heaven *everyone* will be happy—poor Sissy and all! Only I *do* wish Sissy to be happy out of heaven first. Oh! I *do* wish Sissy to be happy!"

Thus Miranda's thoughts ran on from one thing to another; but, run on as they might, they were all as sweet and bright and innocent as her face.

Presently Mrs. Green came into the room, bringing her scanty repast—a bit of cold mutton and a potato.

"My dear," said she, " I fetched a cup of tea up to Miss Sophy, and she's taken it and a morsel of toast, and now she's gone to sleep again. Poor thing! she's tired out; and if I believe in Adam, Miss Miranda, I believe that tired out is just the only thing that's the matter with her; I do, indeed."

"Well, I must work double, then, and try to rest her," said Miranda, cheerfully. "I like working double—it makes me feel strong and big."

"Bless your innocent heart," said the landlady; "eat your dinner, and don't tire yourself out too. That's the best thing to do the poor body up stairs good, or to make you big and strong either."

Then Miranda ate her dinner, and Mrs. Green waited on her.

"My dear," said she, confidentially, "that's a queer gent we've got on our first floor."

Miranda blushed crimson and laughed softly.

"He's been and saw a ghost immediate," said Mrs. Green; "and no one ever see'd a ghost on these premises before—not in any number of weeks, let alone the first evening."

Miranda opened her eyes wide.

"What was the ghost like?" asked she.

"Like a pretty woman, he says, dressed all in white—but, in course, it was dressed in white—that follows, for ghosts always is; it would be unnatural like if they wasn't, in course."

"And what did it do?"

"Well, it appeared—and it couldn't help that neither—there's not much fault to be found with it for that; for, *as* a ghost, it could not do much else, I suppose."

"And was that all?"

"Dear me, no; that wasn't all, miss. It did what no ghost has any call to do that I ever heared tell of—it blew out the candle."

"Good gracious, Mrs. Green! what a thing for a ghost to do!"

"Well, leastways, miss, the candle went out somehow—the thing appeared, and the candle went out—and then the first floor struck a light, he did, and sees the white thing just whisking through the door; and he follers it, he does, and finds nothing at all, nowhere."

"And did he really believe it was a ghost?"

"Not at first, miss. He questioned me as to every woman there was in the house, and I told him there was myself and the cook and Nancy; and he sniggered, the first floor did, and he says, says he, it wasn't none of we; so I said there was Mrs. Jones and the two Miss Jones's in the front parlor; so he questions me about them sharp, and I tells him Mrs. Jones is a fine woman of forty-five, and the Miss Jones's are her husband's sisters, and no younger than she, and just like other ladies who don't get married when they are young; so he sniggered again, the first floor did—he's a one for sniggering, he is—and he says it wasn't them at all; and I says, says I, of course it wasn't, or anyone else neither, but just that he'd fallen asleep on his sopha and dreamt it; and then he asks, the first floor does, is there nobody else in the house at all; and I says nobody at all; and then I tells him of you and Miss Sophy, and that you'd both been in your bed for hours and hours and hours when he came home; and then he says, says he, very well, then, of course it must have been a ghost, for it was nobody at all, and he'd seen it evident; and he never slept on the sopha, and wouldn't have such a thing evened to him; and he never took a drop too much, and he hadn't had a drop then at all, and he hoped he could stand a great deal more than he'd took *that* evening without seeing ghosts; so I just said, more shame for him, and left him there. But I'm afraid he's wild, Miss Miranda, and I shall give him notice to quit if it happens again, for I couldn't have ghosts seen in my house—it might give it a bad name—and, for my own part, I can't abide the creatures, and never could."

"Oh dear, Mrs. Green!" said Miranda, quite

alarmed; "I wouldn't give the poor man notice to quit on that account—I wouldn't, indeed. Probably nothing more will happen; and it would be very hard upon him—very."

"Then why does he go for to see ghosts, miss?" replied Mrs. Green, with unusual sharpness.

For two days Miranda nursed Sophy assiduously, working by her bedside, and never leaving the house. And just as brave and cheerful was she as if she lived in a gay, happy home the life of pleasant ease led by the generality of young ladies in England. On the afternoon of the second day she was obliged to leave her sister to go to Madame La Gai's show-rooms. Occasionally, Sophy was expected to appear in the show-rooms—an employment which she always kept to herself, and in which she never allowed Miranda to assist; but to-day there was no help for it; Sophy could not go, and so Miranda must.

To tell the truth, she rather liked the idea—there was novelty in it—change and variety; and though Miranda never found herself consciously wishing for change, she welcomed it, when it came, with delight.

She put on the black silk skirt in which Sophy

usually attired herself for these occasions, and her own little Sunday bonnet, which, thanks to the fashion of bonnets, was as pretty, foolish, and becoming as the most expensive head-dress turned out by Madame Elise could probably be, though it had been made by her own fingers, at the cost of a few shillings.

She smiled at herself in the glass.

"You don't look half so pretty, dear," said she, "as you did in diamonds and white satin ; but *that* doesn't matter. You are *not* going to dance, and "— with a little pause and a little sigh, and an almost reluctant dwelling on the words—"you *won't* meet Lady Gregory's nephew." And so she kissed Sophy with the tenderest kisses, and, tripping out of the house, sought Madame La˙ Gai's handsome private residence in George Street.

When she went up into the bonnet and mantle room, the first person her eye rested on was a tall, slight, fashionable-looking lady, with a dark, cross, ugly face.

"Who is she?" thought Miranda. "I know I have seen her before. Who can she be ? Oh ! is it possible ? Yes, to be sure—poor, plain thing ! — it really is Miss Hitchcock. How cross she looks !

What a *horrid* fellow Mr. Cressingham *must* be to marry her! Oh! I had fifty thousand times rather be my poor, little, young, hard-worked self than that rich, ill-tempered woman who is going to be married for her money."

"Put it on that young person's shoulders," said a remarkably pleasant voice, that quite took Miranda by surprise, proceeding as it did from the cross, plain face she was passing her reflections on. "Put it on that young person's shoulders; she has a tolerable figure, and one might judge better of the effect."

So Miranda, quite new to the work as she was, was turned round, blushing and surprised, to have an exquisite little bit of furbelow and froth—in which lace, gauze, and ribbon somehow managed to keep together, and to make a sort of a something which might adorn, though it could neither warm nor conceal the figure—thrown over her slight graceful shoulders.

Miss Hitchcock put up her glass, and desired her to move about, while she scanned the furbelow and froth criticisingly, but with evident satisfaction.

"Yes," she said, slowly, in the same pleasant voice; "it's not so bad—it may do—there's something rather novel and nice about it, isn't there?" Then, suddenly bringing her eye-glass to a halt on Miranda's fair, blushing face, and with a puzzled expression on her own—"Have I seen that young woman here before, Madame La Gai?"

"No, ma'am, I think not," replied Madame La Gai, slightly annoyed, and casting an apologetic glance at Miranda.

"Her face seems strangely familiar to me. A likeness, I suppose."

"She is like Miss Venables," said a lady who accompanied Miss Hitchcock.

"Oh no, mamma!" cried another; "she is the very image of that pretty girl at Lady Gregory's ball whom Mr. ——"

"Hush Maria," said the elder lady.

"Yes," said Miss Hitchcock, slowly, and letting her glass drop from her eye, " that must be the likeness I saw. But why should Maria hush, Mrs. Leslie? Do you think I mind?" And she gave a harsh, scornful laugh, as strikingly unpleasant as her voice was the reverse.

Meantime, Miranda stood blushing and out of countenance, but so much amused, that her pretty dimples were constantly appearing.

"Certainly," said Maria, smiling kindly at her, "it is the strongest likeness I ever saw. You don't mind being considered like a great beauty who made quite a sensation at Lady Gregory's ball," she added, addressing Miranda in a tone of pleasant patronage; "do you?"

"But I'm not a beauty, am I?" exclaimed Miranda.

"Well, indeed, I think you are," replied the other girl, laughing. "I'd give a good deal, I can tell you, to have such a complexion as yours, without pink and white polish."

"Don't be foolish, Maria," said her mother; "don't be putting ideas into the young woman's head."

"But what's the use of heads, mamma, unless we have ideas in them? and what the use of ideas unless they make us jolly? and there's nothing going so awfully jolly as knowing we are pretty," said Maria, a delicate, fragile little beauty, who looked quite unfit to utter the slang phrases that tripped cheerfully out of her small rosebud mouth.

"What was that girl's name at Lady Gregory's ball?" said Miss Hitchcock.

"I asked everybody, and nobody knew," replied Mrs. Leslie.

"Why didn't you ask nobody then, if nobody knew," said her daughter. "*I* asked nobody, and so I can tell you. She was a Miss Style—a great Yorkshire heiress who came with Mrs. Nesbit. *Isn't* it hard lines on *nous autres* that such a beauty should be an heiress too. I'll bet a pony she sings. Do you sing?" turning abruptly to Miranda.

"Oh yes, I sing," she replied, laughing.

"Oh, mamma! oh, Miss Hitchcock! we've nothing to do till the carriage comes. Do let us make her sing. You'll sing, won't you, you counterpart of Miss Style?"

"Only I'm not an heiress," said Miranda, shaking her head.

"Such a pity, isn't it? But perhaps you will be some day. Some rich old fellow will leave you a fortune, or some rich young fellow will marry you."

"Hush, Maria," said her mother.

"But *mayn't* she sing, mamma? You know how we want a soprano. Wouldn't she just do? She sings soprano, of course."

"How can you be so nonsensical?"

"Well, mamma, if we don't catch such a catch as this, we shall be doing what pulpit men are always telling us *not* to do—what is it? I forget. I have a bad head for words; but it's something or other about—what is it now? It's not *investments*, or *digestion*, is it? No, no; those are the two things papa's always talking of; but you *must* know what I mean, mamma, for your own pet parson was going on at us about it at a precious rate only last Sunday morning. Oh! I beg your pardon. I forgot you were asleep all the time, so you couldn't be expected to remember."

"How could I help dozing a little, my dear, when you kept me at Mrs. Venables' ball till two o'clock the night before?"

"Oh! nobody's blaming you—don't cry out till you're hurt—don't defend yourself till called upon. But I have it! I know what I'm talking about at last—it's *privileges!* Yes, that's what clergymen are always talking about—our privileges! We're not to fly in the face of our privileges—and here's one, and I do declare you're going to fly in its face, mamma—you are, indeed. Now what *is* the use of going to church?"

"My dear, pray do whatever you like," replied her mother, resignedly.

"Oh! very well. I'm glad I've reformed you. A reformed parent is no end of a blessing. Now, my dear, will you sing us a pretty song directly, please, so that we may see if you'll do!"

Miranda stood smiling, and now and then laughing a little, while the young lady was running on. Now she opened her eyes wide and looked about her.

"But am I really to sing?" asked she, her fair face radiant with smiles.

"Yes, indeed, you are, you pretty creature!" cried Maria, laughing admiringly at her in her turn as she spoke.

Miranda almost raised her hand to clasp that of the kindly, fast, fashionable girl, who was looking at her with such friendly eyes; but the impulse was only momentary, and her hand fell by her side again. And then suddenly she burst forth into one of her quaint old-world songs, not at that time known in London circles, but which now, I believe, are to be had at the music-sellers' shops in Regent Street.

MIRANDA'S SONG.

"Where are the words so sweet and gay?
  Alas! where are they hidden?
The words my lips were meant to say?
  O for the glory of a day
    When they will come unbidden!

> Those I speak were never meant
> From these lips of mine to spring,
> Vaguely bringing discontent—
> And that is all they bring!
>
> "Why do I utter word on word,
> Invented and amended?
> O for the instinct of a bird,
> Who sings not what is most preferred,
> But what was first intended!
> All its joy I covet not—
> Happy nest and plumage gay—
> Could I only utter what
> I were meant to say!"

For a few minutes the room was full of the exquisite music and the strange suggestive words that floated about among bonnets and head-dresses, *robes de chambres* and promenade dresses, like mountain breezes in a ballroom.

After that there was a profound silence.

The three fashionable women stood looking at Miranda, and saying not a word.

At last Maria spoke.

"Oh, mamma!" she cried, "it's heaven, isn't it? We *must* have her for our charade."

It was a curious jumble of ideas, perhaps—heaven and our charade—but Maria's sweet, fragile face expressed some deeper emotion than was wont to shine there.

" Indeed, my dear, I think we must," replied Mrs. Leslie. " What do you say, Miss Hitchcock?"

Miss Hitchcock said nothing. She had tears on her cheeks.

Miranda felt her gay heart almost dismayed as she saw the brown, hard, ugly woman crying at her song.

" Perhaps," said she, softly, " she is the best of us all."

The others did not attend to her.

" You will have to come to us?" cried Maria. " You see mamma says so too. You *will* come, won't you?"

" But what am I to come for?"

" Oh! to be soprano in our charade. Our soprano has gone abroad, and we won't know what on earth to do without one, and you are such an awfully nice little thing."

" Am I really?" asked Miranda, simply. " I didn't know it."

" Yes, but you are; and you sing like a bird; and you've a very good form, too, and altogether very like an angel."

" I really think, if the young person will give us

her address," said Mrs. Leslie, "that some arrangement might be made."

"Why, you live here with Madame La Gai, don't you?" said Maria.

"No," replied Miranda, "I live with Sophy."

"Happy Sophy!" said the London belle. "I should like to live with you, my dear; and if I was a man, I'd marry you to-morrow."

"Yes, if I would marry you," laughed Miranda, confident in her maiden freedóm; "and Sophy is not one bit happy. She is ill now, and she is not happy even when she is well."

"Are we to stay here all day?" asked Miss Hitchcock, very abruptly.

"I thought we were waiting for—" began Mrs. Leslie.

"I am not waiting for anyone," replied Miss Hitchcock, haughtily; "and I never shall think of waiting for *him*. I made an appointment, which I kept because I always keep my appointments; but if other people don't, *I* don't wait. I have finished my business. Shall we go?"

Her harsh words were spoken in her peculiarly pleasant voice, and ended by a slight unmirthful laugh, as harsh as themselves.

"Oh yes, certainly, by all means," replied Mrs. Leslie, a little flurried. .

"But where do you live, my dear?" said Maria, addressing Miranda.

Miranda gave her direction, which the young lady wrote carefully down on the outside of her ivory fan.

"Well," she said, "I shall either send for you to me, or I shall come to you, and then we can settle everything, can't we?"

"Yes, certainly," said Miranda, laughing, "I suppose we can."

"What a joyous thing you are!" said Maria, rather enviously. "Are you always laughing?"

"Yes, generally, I think," was the reply, with another happy little laugh, "when I'm not doing something else."

And so the three ladies swept out of the room, and the young dressmaker remained alone.

She moved mechanically into the window, and watched Maria and her companions get into a very handsome carriage and drive away.

"How curious it all is!" thought she, dreamily. "Have I somehow got into a new world since the moment when I walked down our door-steps in Miss

Hitchcock's wedding dress? Is it all different, and always to be different? and will the old monotonous days never return? First the ball—now meeting them here, and that Maria making me sing—and this charade they talk of; will that be the next thing, or will there be anything else between now and then? We must not get dull again, my life; must we, you and I? But were we dull before? You were, I do believe; but was I? No. I wasn't one bit; but shall I be now, if we both went back again to the old thing? Yes, I shall—and that's how it has been. Now I understand poor Sophy. She is unhappy because she knows; and I didn't know, and now I do. There was no merit in my being gay, but there would have been in her being so. It's like what papa—dear papa—used to say about courage—it's nothing at all unless you know what the danger is; in fact, you are not really courageous unless you are frightened—that's only a way of putting it, of course; but you must see and appreciate the danger before you can show true courage. And now, what I have got to do is to be cheerful and happy, though my eyes are opened, and I *know* what my life is, and what it might be— if I'm not, all my gay spirits were mere selfishness, and worse than worthless—that will be a sort of courage, and I believe I can do it. I feel brave, and I love Sophy." And if ever a young creature looked at once brave and loving, thus looked our Miranda, as she stood in that window, her cheeks rather pinker, and her eyes more radiant than usual, as her pure, beautiful soul, full of these new thoughts, shone through them. Unconsciously, she was gazing into the streets all the time, and unconsciously the words came floating back into her mind with hardly their full sense attached to them —" But will the charade be the next thing? or will there be something else between this and then?" She was fully awakened to her meaning by what did happen at that very moment.

A cabriolet, with a splendid horse in it, and with all its appointments, as even her ignorant eyes could see, in the first style, dashed up to the door beneath her window, and, flinging the reins to his groom, while the bright bay charger stood almost upright on his hind legs with the sudden shock of the halt, Lady Gregory's nephew jumped out of it.

"Was he come as an answer to her thoughts?" Blushing deeply—of course only from the surprise

—and with her heart beating rapidly—of course from the same cause alone—Miranda drew back into the room.

"He is not coming in here, I know," she said, softly.

CHAPTER IV.

A TÊTE-À-TÊTE.

AND at the same moment he entered the room. He had a discontented, irritated air about him, which did not prevent her noticing—perhaps for the first time—how handsome he was. She even thought that slightly weary, slightly scornful look suited his pale face and finely-cut features. He glanced round him.

"No one here?" he said, just aloud; then his eye fell on her.

"Good gracious!" he exclaimed; not a very elegant or refined salutation, it must be confessed, but in its genuineness, and in the voice in which it was spoken, expressing volumes. And then his face lighted up in the most extraordinary manner. Unaffected joy took possession of it, and a dark-red color actually mounted into his pale cheeks.

There could be no doubt that the man was both astonished and delighted.

"And all at seeing *me!*" thought Miranda. "How *very* nice!"

"Is it you? Is it possible?" cried he. "How little I thought, when I mounted those stairs—most unwillingly, I admit—that each step I took was bringing me nearer to your presence."

"Of course, you didn't think it," replied she, smiling.

"Yes; but why?" he cried. "I contend that I ought—that it is hard on me that I didn't—that we *ought* to have instincts and perceptions, and that it is unfair to ourselves, when our hearts are so full of them, if we have none outside our hearts."

"I wonder whether *I* had," said she, a little thoughtfully; "and that what I was thinking at the moment you drove up meant it."

She had not the faintest idea of all, or any, of what this speech committed her to. He saw that, or the look of joy with which he received it would have been dashed with disapproval, and perhaps the whole course of both their lives might have been changed only by that one speech.

But in her utter unconsciousness lay her charm, and to the man of society that charm was deep and potent.

A TÊTE-À-TÊTE. 77

The little mantelet, all furbelow and froth, still hung on her shoulders, and her bonnet, as I have before said, would pass muster anywhere. She looked like a fashionable girl with the face and spirit of an angel—though as angels *are* spirits, I suppose they cannot correctly be said themselves to possess what they are.

"I have been looking for you everywhere," said Lady Gregory's nephew—"at the opera, in the park, and all in vain; and then I find you *here*, when I am neither looking for you nor expecting to find you."

"Yes," she said, smiling, "but that is so often the case, isn't it? The things come, when we are *not* thinking about them, so much more frequently than when we are."

"It would be difficult for *you* to come when I am not thinking of you," said he; and the remark might pass for one of easy gallantry with those who did not know the man, and so could not perceive how much he was in earnest.

"Was not that ball charming?" said she, with some abruptness, but only because her mind was still full of the ball.

"Yes," he replied, "it was *the* most charming ball I ever attended."

"And you have been at so many," said Miranda, with almost a sigh; "and that is my only one. How odd it must seem to have been to a great many balls."

"But you will go to a great many too," answered he, with quite a smile. "Have not you been to any since?"

She pursed up her mouth demurely, and glanced at him from under her long lashes.

"No," she said, emphatically, "not to one. Isn't it odd?"

"But you will," he said; "and they will become mere commonplaces in your life, and at last be regarded as necessary troubles; while before that— while you are still enjoying them—that first ball will fade away into something poor and insignificant."

"Yes, that is likely, isn't it?" cried she, indignantly. "That would be mere ingratitude. I think it is so mean and ungrateful to feel in that way about things that did all they could for you at the time, because other happy things have happened since."

"And yet we all do, don't we?" said he.

"No, we all don't—I don't. I love all my childish treats still, just because they were such treats then."

"Do you really?—cowslip balls, donkey rides, and everything?"

"Yes, I do. You laugh at me, but I don't care. I won't despise one of them. I love everything nice that ever happened to me. I think I love them all the more because I shouldn't care for them now; because—ah! I'm stupid, and can't express what I mean, but anybody must understand it. You do, don't you? *Don't* you feel it too?"

What man could have resisted that don't, and those eyes fixed so pathetically upon him? Certainly not Lady Gregory's nephew. Perhaps there was nothing in the world he would not have declared he understood and felt, if so adjured. At all events, he expressed complete and undivided allegiance to the sentiments she now uttered, adding, when he had done so, with a sincere and unwonted humility—

"I have not always thought of pleasures in that light before, but it has been from want of consideration more than from want of understanding. It is a duty of the affections that I recognize the moment it is put before me."

"A duty of the affections?" said she, with an air of examination. "I suppose it is, though it had not occurred to me '" and she gave him the sweetest little look of respect possible. "I like to think of it so."

A thrill of happiness, the intensity of which amazed him, went all through him as he met that glance of bright deference.

"We are *very* different, I suppose," said he; "but see how we feel alike. The difference is in our lives only, perhaps."

"In that very past we were speaking of," replied she, thoughtfully; "it makes all the difference in people, doesn't it?"

"It makes a great difference, but——"

"It is the background. Do you know, I discovered to-day that our backgrounds make *us*."

"You discovered that to-day?"

"Yes; that the figures in a picture come out and look just what their background chooses. You have a background full of balls. How strange it must seem! I have only one ball in my background! Now, you can't *think* how that one ball has changed me. It is like some great light put suddenly into the background of a picture."

"Just a great piece of happiness," said he, smiling.

"Oh no," she replied, shaking her head; "not only that. Did you think that was all!"

"Why, what else is it?"

"The great light in the background does not only make light; it shows *how* dark some of the other parts really are," said she, quite sorrowfully.

He looked at her now with surprise, as he felt how unlike she was to the other girls he knew.

"You are very young," he said, "to have thought so much."

"What! I?" she cried, laughing. "Why, I have never thought at all!"

"Then you are extremely clever."

"Oh no," she said, "*I* am not clever; Sophy is."

"Sophy must be wonderful, if she is cleverer than you are."

"Don't laugh at me. Sophy is everything that anybody could be, or ought to be. She is so good and so poor and so old." This was spoken with quite a little burst of enthusiasm. "Oh! I *am* sorry for Sophy."

"So am I, I'm sure, though I am not accustomed to think much about poor old people. Why do you call her Sophy, if she is so very old? Sophy sounds young, but I suppose she is an aunt, or something of that sort?"

"She is my sister, and she is *ten years* older than I am!"

"Oh—h! I see—she is old in that sort of way! Now I understand. Do you know, you have made me feel quite anxious to make Sophy's acquaintance. Do you think there is any chance that I might be introduced to her?"

But Miranda shook her head, and looked inexorable.

"No," she said, "I don't think there is the slightest."

An expression of great disappointment came into his face.

"I am going to dine at Mrs. Nesbit's on Thursday," he said, in rather an offended manner.

"Are you?"

"Yes. I have not dined there for ages; and I had not meant to go there; but I do so only for the happiness of meeting you." His manner was still that of a person slightly offended.

But Miranda laughed, and made no other reply to his words than by her gay yet gentle laugh.

"And where else shall I meet you?" he asked, earnestly, the shade of hauteur going out of his voice as he looked at her.

"I'm sure I don't know," said she, "unless perhaps, at Mrs. Leslie's charade party."

She could not help saying this; the words suggested themselves to her even while she was speaking, and her tongue uttered them without consulting her brain.

He caught at the idea. "Will you really be there?" he cried, delighted.

"Perhaps," she answered; "I'm not sure, but perhaps I might."

"Then I will certainly go, even on the chance; but I won't perform unless you do. Are you to be among the audience or the performers? You will tell me, won't you?" speaking ingratiatingly; "and then I shall know what to do myself."

"Well, *if* I go," said Miranda, excessively amused, and feeling, while she carried on the jest, as if she was even now taking a part in a charade, the answer to which had yet to be guessed. "*If* I go, I should very probably help them as soprano."

"Oh! you sing?" he said. "That is delightful. I might have guessed that. You look it."

"Maria has asked me to sing," said Miranda, with admirable gravity, and promising herself a hearty fit of laughter as a reward when it was all over, and he was gone.

"They *were* here, then, were they?" asked he, his countenance falling a little, like one to whom some unpleasant reality had suddenly occurred, while the play element in his nature was all aglow.

"Yes, Mrs. Leslie and Maria and Miss Hitchcock."

"Ah well! never mind; they are gone; let them go." Was he speaking to himself or to her?

"With all my heart," said she, laughing.

"Do you know," he said, "what it is to be very abruptly wakened out of a very happy dream?"

"The dazed feeling?" said she. "Oh yes!"

"And the instantaneous bitter certainty that it *is* only a dream, and that you *are* awake. No consolatory doubt—no blessed indecision. There is your life—you must take it up; there is your dream—you must leave it behind you."

"No," she said, instantly; "I don't know that feeling. Dreams, whether waking or sleeping ones, continue part of us. We can't undream them. We are roused out of them, but they remain."

"Do they?" he said, doubtfully. "Yes, I really believe they do—part of our background. Say— are not they?"

She nodded her head. "Yes," she said, "I believe they are."

"And perhaps," he added, "if we tried very hard, we could make them realities."

"If we dream *very* much, we sometimes fulfil our dreams," said she, smiling brightly. "They make us *do* things; at least day-dreams—castles in the air— do. But for them I should never—" have been at that ball, she was going to say; but she stopped herself just in time.

"After all, a man can make his own life," said he, looking steadily at her. "His life is in his own hands in great measure—in all essentials—at least till he marries."

"Ah! it must be great to be a man. Would not I fashion a noble life for myself!"

"Would you?" cried he, catching her enthusiasm. "And so would I; and so *will* I. From this moment I have taken my resolution. I intend to be happy."

"Well I suppose men can even be happy if they please—if they set about it the right way; but women can't set about—they are at the mercy of almost everything."

"But then the happiest thing of all that a man has to do, is to make a woman happy."

"Yes," she said, smiling; but her maidenly instincts forbade her pursuing that branch of the subject.

"When I said a man could make his own life, you said that was great," he continued, looking steadily at her, "and you said it with shining eyes; but when I spoke of being happy, disappointment came into your face. Why?"

"Oh!" she said, "of course; because it was *only* being happy."

"Only! But what can you mean? Is not that what we are all trying for, and all failing in? more's the pity. The great object of our lives is that we shall be as happy as we can according to our different tastes and wishes."

"But to be good or great," she cried; "those are the *first* objects, are they not? and then happiness if we can."

"Well, of course," he said, reflecting, "one would not do a wicked thing in order to be happy. I wouldn't steal a purse, if I wanted money ever so much, in order to get it."

"Oh! wouldn't you?" she replied, laughing. "How good you are! And is that all?"

"What do you mean by *all*?"

"Why, if you got money by stealing a purse, it would not make you happy, I fancy, because you have been brought up as a gentleman."

"Well, no; I suppose it wouldn't; but I don't follow you."

"Oh!" she said, "we must *be* good and *feel* nobly about everything before we think of being happy, mustn't we? And it sounded odd when you spoke of making your own life, and then merely said you would be happy. But, of course, you didn't mean it," she added, simply, "and it was stupid of me if I looked disappointed."

His countenance had become very grave.

"It would be easy for anyone to be good and noble who—who lived with you," he cried.

"Why?" she asked, very innocently.

"Oh!" he said, with a sort of impatience, "some women are angels to lead us right, while others are ———" Then he stopped with a sound that resembled a groan more than anything else.

"We all have our angels," she answered, smiling.

What more might have been said I don't know;

but as Miranda uttered the word " angels," the clock on the mantel-piece struck, and then struck five times more—six in all—and she gave a great start.

"Oh!" she cried, "I must go home."

"Will you disappear as you did when we parted last," he said. "Will you not let me see you home? Is your carriage there? Was it to be really like Cinderella that you disappeared in that cruel way; and you did not even leave me the slipper."

"You forget that I had boots on," she answered, laughing joyously.

"Boots! oh yes, boots!" he cried; "and isn't it always so? Isn't it just the difference between boots or slippers that makes or mars a man's life?"

It was now her turn to be surprised at his sayings.

"But how?" she asked.

"Why thus. I will take an example: I could not find you because you did not leave me a slipper; you did not leave me a slipper because, by mere chance, you wore boots; and by these chances and trifles lives are lost."

He spoke seriously; but she only laughed.

"And so," she said, "everything is a mere chance, and yet you speak of making your own life!"

"True," he answered; "but how can I help it?

If the chances are all straight against him, what is a man to do?"

"I don't believe in chances," she cried, brightly. "When you spoke of boots or slippers making or marring a life, I thought it was because boots meant work, and slippers sloth."

"Thank you," he cried, eagerly; "you have given me the key-note. There is hope in that. Yes; I will *work*. I will use every means to bring about my end."

"But you must wear thicker boots than those," she cried, glancing archly at his feet, "if the work is at all difficult."

"I will wear seven-leagued boots if necessary."

"Ah! there it is; you can't do your work yourself, and you give in at once, and call upon the giants to help you." And she shook her head at him in the prettiest way possible.

The man of the world had never felt as he did now. I suppose his heart was in the right place after all, for it answered at once with delight to nature and goodness. He boldly recognized to himself that he was in love. And when Miranda stood there, smiling and shaking her head at him, he said over and over again, in his own mind, "You shall be my wife."

Suddenly she held out her hand with a sweet, sorrowful face.

"Good-bye," she said ; " I *must* go."

And she was gone, ere his fingers had done more than touch hers, disappearing through a door into an inner room, not by the one that opened on to the public stair, and by which he had entered.

CHAPTER V.

THE FIRST FLOOR.

MIRANDA almost ran home. Her heart reproached her for having idled away too much time, and staying too long from Sophy.

" Conversation is such a delicious thing," she said to herself, " that while one is conversing time flies, and one forgets that it is not going at its usual jog-trot pace."

But I do not think there was *any* jog-trot in Miranda's life. There never is in youth, though youth is not always aware of its own privileges, and sometimes imagines that its lovely monotony is jog-trot.

She was in such haste to return, and entered her home so quickly, that in the passage she almost ran into the arms of a man with a big, bushy black beard, who was about to leave it with equal rapidity.

" Hullo!" cried he; "I beg pardon. Oh, is it

you? You are the young lady in the back parlor, ain't you?"

"Yes," was the almost breathless reply.

" Then you are the very person I want to see."

She looked at him, and colored brightly; while her heart beat fast.

" Are you the first floor?" she said, timidly; for in truth she felt extremely frightened. She believed he had recognized her.

" Yes," he said; "and I am the first floor only because you are the back parlor. I saw you before."

" Oh!" she cried, "I could not help it; let me pass, please."

And she tried to pass him. But his rather stout, thick-set figure filled up the breadth of the passage too completely to leave room on either side of him even for slight Miranda to slip by.

"I saw you in church last Sunday fortnight, and I followed you, and you came in here, and so I took lodgings here."

Then Miranda recovered her self-possession in a moment, and fixed her eyes on him in innocent reproof.

" You were extremely foolish then," she said, her

young voice bright and clear as a bell; "and you have no right to tell me so or to speak to me at all. Please let me pass."

"Stop a moment," he cried. "I am an artist. I am painting a picture. I wanted a face—a particular sort of face. I had been looking for it for weeks, and at last I found it in church. It's you."

"Oh, I beg your pardon!" cried she; "is that all! I really thought you meant a compliment, and that would have been *so* impertinent, you know."

"It's not an impertinent compliment," he answered, "only an artistic one. I'm thinking of my work, not of you."

She laughed. "Oh yes," she said; "I don't mind that at all."

"And will you sit to me?"

"I can't really. I've not time; and I don't know you. I could not sit to you."

"Oh! if that's all. If it's the want of an introduction, I'll soon set that right. Mrs. Green! Mrs. Green!"

And he ran to the top of the back stairs and shouted down them. The worthy landlady appeared at the top of them before Miranda, in her surprise, had thought of going away.

"Mrs. Green, will you introduce me to this young lady?"

"Well really, Mr. Gaunt, I don't know. Why should I?" said she, panting. "Dear heart, sir! I thought you'd see'd another ghost!"

"I'm painting a picture, Mrs. Green, that will make me immortal. I'm stopped for want of a face, and there it is. Won't you be a good woman, and introduce me to it, and come with it into my room while I just make a little, little sketch of it?"

"A picture, sir? Well, Miss Miranda *would* make a pretty picture, to be sure. I can't see why she shouldn't. Miss Miranda, my dear, this gent is the first floor, and I'd the best of references with him, as I always do. Mr. Gaunt, Miss Miranda Maxwell."

And the worthy woman made signals of introduction far more rational than those used in society.

"Well, I *am* blessed!" said the artist; "Miranda too! Who would — who *could* have thought it? Then I *must* be a witch! Why, it's as Miranda I want to take you. Isn't such a coincidence as *that* enough to strike a man all of a heap? Darwin's development is nothing to it — nothing at all."

"Miranda?" cried she, blushing and smiling; "oh no, I'm not half pretty enough for Miranda."

"I'll be hanged," was the reply, "if you're not pretty enough for anything. Beg pardon; I didn't mean it. I'm respectful; I'm per-fect-ly respectful; only somehow the words came of themselves—they did indeed. But I'm per-fect-ly respectful—didn't mean it—only, you see, I'm trembling with impatience to begin. Good gracious! it is *such* a chance; it mightn't occur in a man's lifetime again —it mightn't indeed."

"But my sister is ill, and I must go to her directly."

"Bless your heart, Miss Miranda," put in Mrs. Green, "she's fast asleep; it's all she can do, poor soul, except eat, and she does both wonderful. I gave her a cup of the best beef tea, that I'd made myself, and she just swollered it, she did; and then off she was asleep again; and it's all she wants my dear—sleep and slops—slops and sleep; she's tired out, and she's coming to on sleep and slops as a rational crittur should."

So Miranda, to her own surprise, accompanied the first floor (being in her turn accompanied by their landlady) into his room, and scarcely half-an-hour after she had parted from Lady Gregory's nephew, at Madame La Gai's, found herself sitting for her portrait to the man to whom she had before this appeared as a ghost.

It was only a little sketch he wanted to take, which he could then introduce into his picture ; and if he nursed in secret any bolder design of making her sit to him by-and-by, in his studio, he did not at this time give a hint of it to any one, appearing perfectly content with the concession she had already made.

Mrs. Green knitted away at the stocking she always had on hand, and made an admirable chaperone.

Miranda was not at all inclined to be silent. She was always amused, and she had friendly feelings for everyone who had not given her unmistakable cause for the reverse.

"How pleasant it must be to paint!" said she, brightly.

"It's pleasanter than pleasant," was the cheery reply.

" Now I should like to earn my living that sort of way," continued she ; " then work must be a delight. Fancy the work one has to do being nice in itself! You must look forward to your morning's work when you go to bed at night."

"Of course I do," replied he. "Why not? Is that anything wonderful?"

"I should think so!" said she. "*We* only feel at night, 'Oh! that day's work is over;' and we don't think about the beginning again next day at all, or we could hardly enjoy the leaving off at night."

"Why what *is* your work?" said he, looking at her with some interest.

"Sewing," replied Miranda, laconically. She thought the one word expressed the life without any amplification.

"Sewing!" echoed he, without an atom of pity in his voice; "why, that's woman's painting."

"No indeed," said she, scornfully; "why woman's painting, if tailoring is not man's?"

"Hullo! what's that?" cried the artist.

"Why, women can paint, can't they? and men can sew, or what would they do for coats? Women's painting! Think of Rosa Bonheur! It's that sort of talking that drives women into standing up for their rights, and so becoming even more silly than the men who make them do it!"

"I beg your pardon humbly," said he; I didn't mean any harm. I didn't want to rile you. Turn your chin up a little. Don't look angry please; and keep your eyelids steady half way down. There, that'll do. Now talk as much as you like. What's it all about? Oh! you paint, do you?"

"No, I don't paint," said she smiling; "and I don't know why I talked so. But I was thinking—couldn't one earn money by music as well as painting?"

"I should think so, rather, *that* one could—jollily. Look at Sims Reeves and old Mario."

"But I'm speaking about women."

"Very well speak of women—bless 'em."

"I have sung all my life, and to-day I've learned I sing well, and I hadn't a notion of it before. Now *do* you think I could earn my livelihood by singing?"

"Sing!" cried he, suddenly interested. "Oh! you sing, do you? Of course you do; what an ass I was not to think of it. It's just the thing—of course it is. Now you see your face is changing every minute, and so I can't catch the expression I want; but singing will do it—that'll keep it steady. I know just how you must look when you're singing; and it's just your singing look that I want. Please, sing a song directly."

"I don't think I can," said Miranda, suddenly turning shy.

"Oh, please, do. Don't think about it; begin all of a heap. Why not? Mrs. Green, won't you make the young lady sing? She must, really. I can't get on at all without it. I can't indeed."

"Do sing one of them pretty things, Miss Miranda, my dear," said Mrs. Green. "Many a time I've stood on the stairs to hear you sing about the green in the sky. Do, my dear."

"The green in my eye!" said the artist, irreverently, but in a very low voice.

"Sing about the green in the sky. Do now, Miss Miranda," urged the landlady.

"You'll find it much easier to sit singing," said the artist, very much as if he was coaxing a hen.

"Oh, well; it's not worth refusing," said Miranda; and so she sang—

"IT IS ONLY.

"There are lakes in the sky
   Of a delicate green;
Had I wings, I would fly
   Where no mortal hath been.
It is only at sunset
   Those lakes can be seen.

"There are forms in the fire,
   There is many a face;
In my heart I aspire

To their tremulous grace.
It is only by twilight
Their wonders I trace.

"There are lights through the trees
On the glittering ground;
And they sway with the breeze,
Keeping time to its sound.
It is only 'mid shadows
Such lights can be found.

"There are joys, deep and true,
Time can bring us alone;
When the morning is new
They are far and unknown.
It is only through sorrow
Such joys are our own."

She stopped there, and Mr. Gaunt, who had been sketching vigorously all the time, with his eyes now fixed on her, now turned to his paper—gave a deep sigh as she did so. He bent over his work without a glance or a thought for the original. His soul seemed in his face, looking with desperate eagerness for the soul in the face before him.

"I've done it!" he cried; "it's perfect! Music for ever! Oh! that blessed song! I knew it would."

Then he began to remember the living Miranda.

He gave her an odd look and smile, and beckoned to her to approach him.

"Come," he said, "and see yourself—it's only fair that you should see yourself."

"I sha'n't like it, I know," said she; and she went across the room and peeped over his shoulder. He was writing on the paper beneath the drawing.

"Oh!" she cried, "I am not pretty like *that*. I wish I was. How could you make such a sweet thing out of *me*, I wonder?"

"Did you ever see yourself sing?" asked he, with a droll, quaint look.

"Well, no, of course, I never did. How could I?"

"Ah! but that's just it—that's how you look while you're singing—it is indeed."

"In that case," cried she, laughing and blushing, "I had better always sing."

"Upon my life," answered he, "I quite agree with you."

"I shall read the 'Tempest' over again directly," said Miranda.

"Have you got it?" asked he, surprised.

"Oh yes," she replied; "we kept a few books. We could not part with Shakespeare, you know."

"Oh!" he said, glancing rather inquiringly from

her to Mrs. Green and back again; "I think I see." Then he added briskly, "If you want to earn your livelihood by singing, I believe you could do it."

"Could I?"

"Yes, I think so; but I'm not sure. I'd like a better judge than I am to hear you. I think you might teach, and I think you might produce a great effect at London parties. I shouldn't like you to sing at concerts. But those two are safe branches, and I think you could do pretty well in both."

"I'm afraid I couldn't teach," said she; "I don't sing scientifically enough. But I might teach *playing* perhaps."

She expressed no surprise—because she felt none—at the interest in her he evinced, by saying he should not like her to sing at concerts. It seemed quite natural to her that everybody *should* feel a kindly interest in everybody else. She cared for all her fellow-creatures, and the feelings her fresh beauty and charming ways excited in those she came in contact with she set down unhesitatingly to a necessary and universal philanthropy.

Mrs. Green regarded the drawing very approvingly. She screwed up her eyes to see it from a little distance, and put on her spectacles to do full honor to a nearer view. What she beheld was this :—

A slight pencil sketch of a young girl, standing on the sea-shore, with innocent, wide-opened eyes looking forward, and a face all alight with a sort of joyful surprise. Under it was written the words—

> "My prime request
> Which I do last pronounce is—Oh! you wonder
> If you be made or no?"

" Dear heart," said Mrs. Green, "it's a nice scrawl, but it's only a scrawl; and, Lor'! what nonsense the words are. Prime! well, to be sure, it makes one think of mutton. Won't you do her in paint, sir?" she added, anxiously.

"Oh yes," he said, laughing, "I shall certainly do her in paint. This is only just the sketch of the figure to be introduced into my picture—my great picture, Mrs. Green, which is to make me immortal. Some day soon I shall ask you to bring the young lady to my studio, as I shall want one, or perhaps two, sittings from her just for finishing all up; and then I'll show it to you, and all my other great pictures too."

"That will be delightful," cried Miranda, with the

glee of a child who finds herself being promised an unexpected treat.

"Did you really come off a desert island, I wonder?" said he, looking at her with his droll, but kindly smile.

"My back room is a desert island," she answered, laughing, "and everything beyond it seems new and charming."

"And now, miss," said her chaperone, "I must go back to my kitchen. Nancy is that stupid she never can dish up properly without me, and the front parlor is awful particklar about their dinners. I'd rather send you or the first floor (with a little sign at Mr. Gaunt) up fifty dinners than them Jones's one."

"And I thought to go to poor Sophy," said Miranda; "if she's awake, she'll want me; and," sighing, "I've got a mantle to trim." Then she turned to Mr. Gaunt, and said warmly and earnestly, "Good-bye; thank you so very much."

"But what for?" he cried briskly, and with amusement; "it's you have been doing me the favor, isn't it? not I you."

"Why, so it is," cried she, laughing; "but I had quite forgotten *that*, because it has been so very delightful."

And so saying, she tripped lightly out of the room, followed by Mrs. Green, who, however, first performed a voluminous curtsey, and took a respectful leave of her first floor.

"That's a very nice party, Miss Miranda," she remarked as they went down stairs together, "and a thorough gent; and if he do choose to see a ghost now and then, in a small way, I almost think I'll make no objections."

"That will be very wise of you, I'm sure, Mrs. Green."

"You see, miss, it wasn't a noisy ghost, and it wasn't a nasty ghost. I can't abide 'em when they're noisy or nasty; and there's no call why I should. But it had no blood about it—leastways he did not say so—and it didn't rattle chains; it seemed a quiet, innocent sort, and maybe it's best not to be over particklar, Miss Miranda."

"I quite agree with you; I think it was one of the most harmless ghosts I ever heard of in my life."

"No, really; was it now, miss? Well, I'm glad you think so too. And I like that first floor uncommon—I do indeed—a gent like that *is* so little trouble. I'd rather let my house to 'em all through than to them Jones's. And he's paid me his week reg'lar as clock-work, and given me a pound to keep in hand for things wanted. I like that first floor uncommon, Miss Miranda; I do indeed."

Then Miranda took her work, and stitched busily late into the night by the bedside of her sleeping sister. She felt as if she had been wasting her time dreadfully; the whole afternoon had been spent in amusement. To be sure, Madame La Gai always gave something for the hours employed at her house, and if few customers had come in, it was not Miranda's fault; still she felt like a truant from school, and that it was her duty now to make up as well as she could for lost time. Sophy slept heavily, and Miranda worked on till one o'clock struck, and she found her thoughts getting confused, and her little head nodding wearily down on to her hands.

The next morning she awoke quite refreshed. She was so young and strong, and had such a young, strong spirit within her, that after a few hours' sleep, she always rose as gay as a lark. Her first waking thought was, to her, a very unusual one—Will anything pleasant happen to-day? "But if it doesn't," she said to herself, "I should be most ungrateful to mind; I must not let pleasure spoil me; I must remember all poor papa said when I was such a silly that I cried because it rained and I couldn't go to the pic-nic. If we regret pleasures, and want them when they don't come, we turn them into pains and that is very foolish, as well as very ungrateful. I remember when Sophy was so vexed because it was a bad year for roses, and she kept mourning over it, and going on about how splendid they had been the summer before, till papa said she was making a past joy into a present grief, and that it would have been better—to hear her talk—if the roses had not given us such a splendid harvest last June. The beautiful roses; I ran out into the garden and kissed them, and begged their pardon for all Sophy had said, the dears! Oh! I do think a bunch of roses would cure Sophy now—poor, *poor* Sophy! I know what I'll do," cried she aloud, with a sudden blush of vivid delight ; " I'll go without my dinner ; I'll just eat a nice large hunch of dry bread when I get *too* hungry, and then, with the money I've *not* spent, I'll slip out of the house, and I'll run away off to some flower-place, and I'll buy a beautiful big bunch of roses—a great cluster of roses—all sweet and fresh and lovely—and bring them in to Sophy. Oh! how delicious! who was afraid that there would be no new pleasure to-day?" She laughed a little at that; and then she knelt down, and said her prayers very reverently, but with a smile on her face all the time.

Sophy opened her eyes, and spoke low and in a confused way. At last Miranda made out that she was telling her she was better. "Only," she said, "I have an odd heaviness in my limbs, I can't move them, and my thoughts seem to come slower than ever, and papa used to call me his dear old slow coach even then." Here she gave a faint, sickly smile, more unlike than a frown would have been, to the smile that lighted up Miranda's fair face and danced in her innocent eyes.

She ran up to her and kissed her several times; thinking of the rose-cure all the while, and so delighted about it she hardly knew what to do.

"Never mind, Sissy," she cried, "it's only that you're tired. Mrs. Green said so. You're just to go on eating and sleeping till you're quite well. And you *are* better, for you've not said so many words to me before for these two days, you dear old thing." Here she kissed her again, and Sophy stared at her, and shut her eyes, and fell once more into a heavy sleep.

Miranda spent all that morning working hard. About three o'clock she got "too hungry," and ate her "nice large hunch of dry bread," which, with the prospect of the cluster of roses before her, seemed to her perfectly delicious.

"Hunger *is* the best sauce," said she; "I had no idea *how* nice dry bread was before."

Ah! Miranda, your kind, tender thoughts were a sweeter sauce than hunger. How pretty and how good you looked in that dingy little room, eating your bit of dry bread, and thinking of Sophy and her roses! The poor sick woman had taken some tea and a morsel of toast for her dinner, and was once more asleep. Mrs. Green was beginning to feel uneasy about her, and to fear there must be something more than merely being "tired out" in a state like hers, continuing so long; but Miranda was too inexperienced to feel the least anxiety; besides, were there not the roses? the rose-cure had not been tried yet; who could resist that? certainly not her Sophy.

And so with half-a-crown in her hand, she went out to hunt for roses as happy as a queen—alas! happier than *our* good Queen can ever be again. Let us hope that fortune may deal more kindly with my Miranda, and that in the far-off time she may not look back to these days of poverty and privation as among the happiest in her life.

She found her roses, and triumphantly made her purchase—red, pink, white, almost lilac, buff, yellow, every shade but blue. Have we not, all of us, at some time or other, wished for blue roses? Not so Miranda. She caressed the beautiful creatures with tender, timid touch, as she took them from the hands of the befrizzled and bechignoned and be-everything-that-is-ugly-and-ungraceful young lady who stood behind the counter.

"How glad I am there are no blue roses," said she, softly; "they would be *so* unnatural."

"Blue roses!" cried the girl, astonished. "Lawk-a-mercy! I wish there were; wouldn't they sell? rather."

Miranda shrank back as if she had been hurt. Then she looked at the young lady with pitying eyes.

"Poor thing!" said she to herself. "I wouldn't like to *sell* flowers; I think it must harden the heart."

When she had nearly reached home, Mr. Gaunt crossed the street and joined her.

"Miranda, with her hands full of roses!" cried he. "Beg pardon, I'm not calling you by *your* Christian name, you know, only by *hers;* I'm perfectly respectful."

"Yes," she said, smiling; "I know. But are they not beautiful? They are for poor Sophy—she is so ill. Do you *think* they will do her good? They must, *mustn't* they?"

She spoke so earnestly that I am obliged to have the words put in italics.

"Flowers are very pleasant when you're ill," said he; and that dreamy look came into his eyes, with which one recalls some almost forgotten time, scattered moments of which float pleasantly back into the taxed memory. "Is Sophy *very* ill?"

"Mrs. Green thinks she's just tired out. She is always asleep, except when she is taking a little broth or tea, and she can't move, and says her thoughts are so slow; but for two days I don't think she had *any* thoughts, so she is better."

"I say," said he, "this won't do at all. Look here. I was bred a doctor—apprenticed and taught, and walked the hospitals and everything—but I liked painting bones better than setting them; though, in *my* opinion, every artist *should* be bred a doctor—it teaches you no end of things, you see, that you find of use when you get your brush on canvas. Now Mrs. Green—worthy old soul she is, by-the-bye, but why so fat? Why do worthy old souls, as a general rule, get so *very* fat? However, fat or thin—and it's not of the least consequence which—she has told me all about you; and I don't wish Miss Sophy to be ill; and I'm afraid she will be very ill, if you don't take care. Will you let me see her?"

"Oh, certainly; I suppose so," said Miranda surprised, and beginning to take alarm, oh happy, unanxious youth; "it is very kind of you, I am sure."

"You look so uncommonly kind yourself," said Mr. Gaunt, "that you make other people the same; not that it's much out of the way to try to set a sick woman on her legs again."

"She is so fond of roses," said Miranda, confidentially, "that I think they *must* do her good."

By this time they had reached the house, and Miranda called Mrs. Green up from the kitchen. Some instinct made her feel, without an instant's reflection, that this was a more comfortable proceeding than taking the artist-doctor to Sophy herself, and alone.

"He has walked the hospitals and done everything all right—everything that makes a man medical, you know," she explained; "and he thinks if we don't take care, Sophy will be really very ill; and he wants to see her. He may, mayn't he, Mrs. Green? It is very kind of him, isn't it?"

"Well, to be sure, I *am* glad," said the fat and worthy one; "I was just wishing for a doctor for her. Not that there's anything much astray"— here she winked volumes, in the largest and clearest possible type, at Mr. Gaunt—"but when people is ill, it's always satisfactory like to have a man in to look at them. I always did say so, Miss Miranda, and I'm not agoing to go from it now; no, miss, I'm not."

With which apology for taking a doctor to Miss Sophy, when it was not to be allowed that she was really ill, Mrs. Green ascended the stairs as fast as her breath would allow her, followed by Mr. Gaunt and Miranda.

8

CHAPTER VI.

SUNDAY.

A DARKENED room, and a poor, weary, oldish-looking woman, lying breathing heavily in a very shabby bed. That was all Mr. Gaunt expected to find, but not all he found; for his expectations, unlike expectations in general, proved less than the reality, and he did not feel at all sure that there was not another presence near, waiting (as that presence perhaps always is) to rush in and seize its prey the first possible moment—always waiting, but always kept at bay by youth and health. Alas! there was neither health nor youth here, so he felt that the presence might be drawing very near indeed—that presence which would bring brightness and joy to the poor weary one, and plunge the other girl, in all her brilliancy, into sorrow and despair.

He felt his patient's pulse and her forehead, examined her eyes, asked her a few questions, and then gave an expressive look at Mrs. Green, who winked folio volumes in large type in reply. He said very little, and the two women said nothing, but stood quietly by, Mrs. Green beginning to feel a good deal frightened, and Miranda rejoicing in her serene heart that poor Sophy would now be made well again. After some time they all went out on to the stairs, and then the doctor spoke.

"It is just *this*, you see," he said ; "her nerves are clean gone, and so she's nothing *but* nerves."

"Oh dear!" cried Miranda, "how very odd!"

"Nerves *are* odd," he replied, sharply; "she's in a low nervous state, and she must be got out of it." And he frowned at Miranda as if she was contradicting him. "I'll send some medicine ; give her oceans of beef tea at short intervals," to Mrs. Green, "and bushels of eggs, and a glass of my medicine at twelve and at four every day. It *looks* like senna," he cried, fiercely fixing his eyes with a stare of defiance on Miranda, "but it's *not* senna." Then he added in a whisper to Mrs. Green, "if it tastes *too* much like good old port, put some ginger or some asafœtida into it ; but make her take it anyhow."

"Bless your heart, sir," replied Mrs. Green aloud, "for the best of gents, be the other who he may."

The three separated on the first floor, Mrs. Green going down to her kitchen, and Miranda returning to her sister's room, to work there by her bedside, but first to give her the roses, and ask her, with many kisses, if she did not think the beautiful, bright flowers would *really* make her well.

"Yes, dear," said Sophy, with a vague, foolish smile.

"You are *so* fond of roses; you *know* you are," cried Miranda, quite appealingly.

"They are so pretty," said Sophy, in the same meaningless way; "and *all* these came from my grave."

"From *where?*" cried the other, almost in a scream.

"Didn't they?" said Sophy, still with the foolish smile on her face; "I thought I saw them."

"But where *did* you say?" urged Miranda, entreatingly.

Sophy kept smiling at her in the same way, but said nothing.

"Dear Sophy," cried Miranda, "I didn't hear what you really said; but never mind, I won't tease you. There is such a quantity I've got to tell you if you'd *like* to hear it. Do you think you would?"

"Oh yes," said Sophy, with vague placidity.

"Such a quantity!" repeated Miranda; "*things* have been happening, and things used never to happen. First and foremost, what do you think? I went to a ball next door in Miss Hitchcock's wedding dress!" And she looked full in her sister's face, and spoke with the air of a person who intended to cause a great deal of astonishment.

But Sophy remained quite unruffled.

"Oh yes," was all she said, and in just the same voice and manner as she had uttered the other "Oh yes."

"What! you knew it?" cried Miranda, amazed in her turn. "Oh, you sly thing—oh, you dear old sly thing!" and she kissed her again. Miranda was very fond of kissing Sophy. "So you knew it all the time! And I danced; oh! Sophy, I danced; it *was* delicious."

"I danced too," said Sophy, "with George."

"Ah! poor Sophy, yes, you did, long ago; but don't think about that now. I want to amuse you. Listen to all I have got to tell. I danced with Lady Gregory's nephew, and he's delightful. I met him again to-day at Madame La Gai's; and we have long conversations. What a charming thing conversation is! I'd no idea it was ever anything like *that*. Sometimes it might almost be better than even dancing. And then only think, ladies came in, and they made me sing, and they said I was a soprano, and a beauty; and I *believe, perhaps*, I'm going to sing at their charade party. There was a very nice girl, a little vulgar; but ladies *are* just a *little* vulgar, aren't they, Sophy!"

Miranda paused for a reply, and found that Sophy was fast asleep, with the foolish smile still lingering on her face.

Mrs. Green strictly obeyed all the artist-doctor's orders, and administered eggs, beef tea, and the suspicious medicine—which was *not* senna, and was cautioned against tasting like good old port—at short intervals to her patient. The result of this judicious treatment was, that by the following morning the poor woman seemed better and brighter, and the vague, wandering look had gone out of her eyes.

The following morning was Sunday. Miranda loved Sunday, and no cloistered nun ever said her prayers with more intense devoutness than did that innocent child, as week after week she knelt reverently down in the crowded London church.

Dressed in her simple Sunday finery, with her prayer-book in her hand, and her face as fresh as a field flower, she tripped gayly down the steps and along the street on the day in question. Somebody saw her from his first floor window, where he was contentedly smoking his pipe; and, drawn by the irresistible attractions of youth, beauty, and goodness, somebody came lumbering down the stairs and plunging out of the door to join her ere she was half-way down the street.

"Good-morning, Miranda; not your name, you know—hers," said Mr. Gaunt.

"Oh! is it you?" said she, smiling, and frankly giving him her hand; "how do you do? What a delicious day! *Don't* you love Sunday?"

"H'm! pretty well; yes, of course; uncommon. It's a day of rest, you know."

"It's such a lovely plan," said Miranda, "and so kind!"

"How much?" asked the artist. "Beg pardon; but I don't follow. What is?"

"Why, Sunday, to be sure," cried she; "it is so

kind to make it a *duty*—rest and prayer; and to make them *duties*, when they might be only *pleasures*, you know. Such lovely duties, to be bound to rest and pray one day in every seven. Is it not a beautiful thing?"

"What a good girl you are!" was his only reply, looking very kindly into her radiant face.

"Are you coming to my church?" asked she, smiling.

"I *was* going to mine."

"Which is that?"

"Well, it's the fields, or anywhere I can get to soonest out of the dirt and din."

"Oh! you pray there?" She looked a little serious.

"Did you ever try it?" asked he, with a laugh.

"Instead of church?" she said, still serious and gently shaking her head. "Oh no; I'm not good enough; that only does for quite holy people who are sure of themselves. I want the church with its walls to keep me safe. I couldn't trust myself quite without it."

"If not you, who?" said he laconically; and his words somehow sounded like the translation of an Italian proverb, but I never heard of any proverb, Italian or otherwise, the least like them. "Well,

I'm going to your church, then, to-day. May I go with you?"

She smiled her consent, and they walked on together.

"Sophy is so much better," she said; "and I think it's all your doing. How can we ever thank you enough?"

"Lor' bless you! it's nothing. I like doctoring people. I've a hankering after the old trade yet; it's the best going, but one. If I wasn't a painter, I'd rather be a doctor than a king."

"It's the most useful of the two," said Miranda, with decision.

"Which?" said he; "there's three mentioned. Now, look here, a doctor's more useful than a king, and an artist's more useful than a doctor."

"No, hardly that. I think you *would* have some difficulty in proving that."

"Should I? Difficulty be—hanged! Here goes. Kings would die without doctors, and doctors only make man fit to be painted; moreover, the works of doctors die in the bodies of men, and by painters' works the bodies of men live for ever."

Then he gave himself a great stretch and yawn,

and said, "Hullo! what a lot of nonsense one does talk to women, to be sure, poor souls."

By this time they had reached the church, and were shown by the pew-opener into different seats.

As Miranda, on the completion of the service, was leaving the building, she was surprised at being accosted by a lady; and she was more surprised, when awakened, by being so accosted, from the gentle reverie in which the act of prayer had left her, to perceive that this lady was Miss Hitchcock. Miss Hitchcock, looking as cross and brown as ever, having arrayed herself—by the directions surely of some malicious imp who appeared always ready to direct her taste to what was *most* unbecoming to that cross, brown face—in a pale blue dress, and a tuft of blonde and forget-me-nots on the top of her chignon, by way of a bonnet.

"Can you come to my house, Eaton Square, to-morrow at three?" asked she, in her pleasant voice. "I have some instructions about that mantle I want to give you. Madame La Gai has sent it to me, and there is something not quite right about the fit."

"To your house?" said Miranda; "that would be very nice." Then she added, seeing that Miss Hitchcock was staring at her in haughty surprise.

Oh! I beg your pardon. How stupid I am! Of course I will come, if you wish it."

" Did you ever see the Miss Style they say you are so like, and that you certainly *are* like ? " asked the lady, not in the least relaxing her haughty stare.

Miranda blushed scarlet, and laughed nervously.

" I *really* don't know," she said. " I don't feel quite sure whether they meant me or somebody else." Then suddenly stopping, she blushed deeper and laughed more, but this time it was a laugh of real amusement. " What an idiot I am!" said she.

" Masquerading is a very foolish thing," said Miss Hitchcock.

" She knows!" thought poor Miranda, and she almost wondered how she survived the thought. " What ? " she cried, faintly.

" Oh, never mind," said Miss Hitchcock ; "perhaps you understand me, and if you don't, there's no harm done ; " and so, without another word, she turned down the street and walked away.

" She must know," cried Miranda, almost wringing her hands. There is nothing else she can mean. Oh! I never shall have courage to go to her—never, never."

And yet as the day went on—the long, dull, city

Sunday, spent in Sophy's garret—Miranda, found her thoughts for ever turning to the coming morrow, and the visit to Miss Hitchcock, Eaton Square. The little changes that had recently come into her life made her long for more. She would not call that life dull; she would not allow herself to repine or even to wish; but when a variety was offered to her, she grasped at it eagerly, and was most unwilling to let it go. Thus she felt frightened to death at Miss Hitchcock, and the thought that she had found out that she had gone to that ball and worn her wedding dress kept coming across her mind as something almost too horrid to be true, and she told herself over and over again that she never could muster up courage to go to Eaton Square next day; and yet she really *meant* to go all the time, and had anything happened to prevent her, it would have been a cruel disappointment.

She read to herself and to Sophy, or chatted to and fed the latter during all that long, dull Sunday afternoon and evening; but her thoughts wandered continually to Miss Hitchcock and her wedding dress. Suddenly Sophy called her up to her bedside, and said in a very quiet voice, "Who is that sitting by the table, Miranda?"

"I was sitting there, dear."

"No, not you—I *know* you. I mean the strange lady. You've got a party, I see. My dear, you will never be able to pay for all those candles!"

"There is only one candle, dear Sophy, and nobody in the world here but me. Oh! what *do* you mean!"

"There *is* a strange lady," said Sophy; and she tried to raise her head from the pillow, and tried to bow towards the table in a ghastly sort of way, which sent Miranda flying affrighted down stairs— not this time to Mrs. Green's kitchen, but to the drawing-room on the first floor.

Two men were sitting smoking together at the table, on which stood bottles and glasses.

"She is going mad!" panted Miranda. "Oh! please, come directly. Don't wait a minute."

"Hullo!" cried one of the men.

"Bless us and save us!" said the other.

But both rose, and the one she knew advanced towards her out of the smoke, leaving the other a dim and demon-like figure within it.

"She says there is a strange lady at the table," said Miranda; "and she keeps bowing to her. Oh! don't let her bow to her—please don't;" and she began to cry.

"I won't," said Mr. Gaunt.

His voice rang through the room, and there was support and comfort in its strong, cheery sound that went straight to Miranda's heart. She smiled amid her tears, and taking hold of his great arm in her two white little hands, led him away to the door—he looking down at her with a tender sort of expression, that beamed oddly, but not unbecomingly, from under his shaggy eyebrows, and then glancing over his shoulder at the dim form in the smoke.

"A co-lodger, Ned," said he, "with a sick sister. I've turned sawbones again for the nonce."

"All right, old fellow," replied Ned. "*You* go where glory waits you, and *I'll* finish the bottle—a fair field and no favor. What's the odds as long as you're 'appy!" and he waved his hand jauntily through the smoke at Miranda.

But Miranda was not thinking of him or of Mr. Gaunt, or of anyone but Sophy; and with hurry and alarm in her manner, and the tears still streaming down her cheeks, she ran before her doctor back into Sophy's room.

Sophy was sitting up in the bed, with a rather frightened expression on her face.

"They have all gone away," she said, in a tone of

complaint; "it is very lonely. George might have stayed;" and then she moaned.

"Who is George?" asked Mr. Gaunt.

Sophy gave a little laugh.

"*My* George," she said.

Was she thinking of a lover? poor thing! and looking almost as unfit for love as the old woman in the mine, who fell weeping on the neck of the beautiful lad who had gone to sleep there fifty years ago, and was found with the glory of his youth undimmed by time—that most pathetic story of deathless love, when the two who had once been all the world to each other, meeting at the end of a long life, the one covered with wrinkles, and the other without a line on his smooth face, fill us with wonder as to *how* they will meet in heaven.

"Oh! don't you mind about George," said Mr. Gaunt, cheerfully. "'He's safe enough, but he can't come here till you're better, you know; you're not very well, you see, and all *you've* got to do is to get well as fast as you can. Now *do* be a brick and get well; do, please, be a brick."

Sophy had composed herself in the bed by this time, and the excited look went out of her face. Mr. Gaunt was mixing something in a glass while he was talking (he had given Mrs. Green a few simple medicines for occasional use, and they were in the room ready), which he presently, in a cool, matter-of-fact way, handed to Sophy and bade her drink. She instantly obeyed, and in five minutes more was fast asleep.

"She'll do, bless her poor old heart," said he to Miranda, after watching the calm slumber for a short, silent time. "Who's George?"

"Oh! will she really do?" cried she, clasping her hands, and unconsciously repeating his words. "Oh! she isn't mad!"

"Mad! fiddlesticks—it's just nerves and weakness. She'll be much better to-morrow. I've given her what will make her sleep as sound as a top. Who's George?"

Miranda blushed vividly.

"He was—papa's—curate," said she, in a slow, hesitating manner.

"Hullo!" cried Mr. Gaunt, looking at her keenly; "was he *your* George too?"

"I was a child," said she with dignity.

"And Sophy," cried he, "your sister?"

"We all liked George; he was a brother to us," said frank Miranda, with sudden reticence, when maidenly modesty bade her guard poor Sophy's secret.

" And nothing more to her ? " questioned he, quite unabashed by her manner.

" Does he really think I will tell him of my sister's lover ? " said she to herself, all aglow with indignation.

" He was papa's curate and our dear friend," was her answer, given at once with spirit and reserve.

" Oh ! just as you like ; please yourself," replied Mr. Gaunt, cavalierly ; " only it might just be the saving of her to make him give her a call ; that's all. But just as you like ; it's nothing to me."

" He is in India," said Miranda, and at the same moment melted into tears.

" Oh ! come now, don't cry," said he, quite mollified. " Of course I'm a brute—I always am when I'm tried—only I didn't mean it ; don't you cry—there's a dear. If George is in India, he can't call at No. 14 Denham Street, London, N.W. George can't, and we must just cure Miss Sophy without him. Only the other would have been the easiest way ; that's all."

Miranda smiled through her tears.

" You're an out-and-out angel," said Mr. Gaunt. " I'm never with you but I catch myself looking for the wings. I say, what do you think of such a rough old codger as I am?"

"I think you are very kind," said she laughing.

"No; do you now?" he cried, holding out his hand to her. "Shake hands upon it then, and don't let us misunderstand each other."

Her little, white hand instantly sought his, and nestling down for a moment like a bird was lost to sight in his great one.

"Such a paw as mine is!" cried he, disgusted. "Just look at yours," and he held it up for a moment ere he let her resume it for her own.

"I can't help it," said she; "and I don't wish it to be like that one."

And she glanced at his, and laughed roguishly, while she caressed her own rosy fingers.

"Heaven forbid!" cried he, and laughed too, with a great, hearty haw, haw, haw; then stopped abashed, looked at Sophy, and said, "Don't."

"I didn't," said Miranda.

"Oh yes, but you did, though," said he; "it was your doing, you know. And you needn't mind; she won't wake easy—she'll sleep hard."

"And now," said Miranda, "don't you think you'd better go away?"

She spoke coaxingly, and looked enchanting.

"Oh yes," said he, with a sort of good-natured crossness; "of course I had. I've been of no use, and now I may go—suck the orange and throw it away, hey?"

"Oh no," said she, laughing; "I hope the orange will roll back again, and find Sophy better tomorrow."

"Good-night, and God bless you!" said Mr. Gaunt, fervently, and he was gone.

"How kind people are," thought Miranda; "how kind everybody is; oh! it is such a nice world;" and so she went to bed and slept as soundly as Sophy, without a sleeping draught.

The next day Sophy was better.

Miranda worked hard all the morning, and then ate her early solitary dinner. Her watch was too fast, and she arrived at Eaton Square at a quarter past two, instead of at three o'clock. The consequence was that Miss Hitchcock had not returned from a luncheon party at a friend's, and that Miss Hitchcock's maid had taken the opportunity of her mistress's absence to absent herself also; and the consequence of *this* was that the footman having received no orders what to do with Miranda, and taking her for a young lady, showed her straight up into the back drawing-room, where she found herself face to face and *tête-à-tête* with Lady Gregory's nephew.

CHAPTER VII.

FRIENDSHIP.

THEY stared at each other.

"Is it possible!" cried Miranda, in accents of delight.

But if she was delighted, what was he? He looked, at first, as if he did not believe his eyes or his senses. Then an expression of actual gratitude rushed into his face, and then one of rapture.

"It is you?" he cried, and took both her hands in his, and gazed down at her fair face till it—at first raised so frankly to his—was turned away, covered with blushes.

There was a moment's silence, and then he dropped her hands and spoke with an odd, forced calmness.

"Do you know," he said, "I thought I had lost you?"

"But why?" replied she, a little shyly. "Why, did you not expect we should meet again?"

"Why did you play me such tricks, then?"

Then she began to laugh, but to blush at the same time very bright.

"Oh!" she cried, "have you really found it out?"

"Have I really found it out? Of course I have," replied he; "how could I help finding it out? I dined at Mrs. Nesbit's on Thursday, as I told you I would. Dull dinners she always gives, and nothing could have induced me to enter the house, as I also told you, except the idea of meeting *you*; and then the first thing I hear is, that you left her the morning after my aunt's ball. Where are you staying?"

He spoke in the tone of a spoiled child, or—shall we say?—a "curled darling," who naturally resented the ruffling of a single rose-leaf under his feet.

"*What* did she tell you?" was Miranda's only reply.

"Well, I did not give you up till dinner was actually announced. Of course"—in a tone of great ill-usage—"I had to take Mrs. Nesbit in, and then"—as if it was a still greater injury—"I didn't even know your name; so after feeling about in the dark a little, and gaining nothing by it, I asked boldly what had become of the young lady she had taken to the ball with her?"

"And *what* did she say?"

"Why, what could she say, but that you had left her next morning?"

"No! did she really?"

"Oh! you had primed her with some stories, had you? she was in the great plot, was she? Well, then, let me warn you against her. She is a traitor; she answered me in the simplest manner, as if I had asked her the merest everyday question; and when I ventured a step further, and inquired your name, she told me it was—"

"What?" cried Miranda, breathless.

"Style."

Miranda looked at him with wide-opened eyes for half-a-second, after which she made a slight movement, as if she was then and there going to begin to dance, but, instead thereof, sank into a chair, and abandoned herself to a fit of laughter—the sweetest, the merriest, and the most inextinguishable that, it appeared to Lady Gregory's nephew, he had ever heard.

He could hardly resist joining in it himself, and yet, somehow or other, this very laughter seemed an injury to him.

"Have not you laughed enough?" said he at last,

discontentedly. "I am sure I have not the slightest idea what there is to laugh at, at all."

"No," said she, "of course you have not; *that* is what makes it so amusing. Don't you see it would be nothing without *that?*"

"Oh! very well," he replied, "but it's rather waste of time, isn't it? We have just these few minutes to be together, and you do nothing but laugh. That woman will be here directly."

"What! Mrs. Nesbit?" cried Miranda, affrighted.

"No, no! of course not; I mean Miss Hitchcock."

"Well, as it's her own house," said she, smiling, "it's hard to speak of her in that voice for coming into it, isn't it? I think she has a right to do *that.*"

"I don't know," he replied. "There seems to me, just at present, to be *no* rights, except those of one soul over another."

"What do you mean?"

"Why, this; when two people meet—but I'm not sure whether it's wise to tell you."

"Oh yes; it's wise to tell me anything."

"Is it? I wish I was certain of that."

"Well, at all events, it's wise to tell me anything I want to hear."

"I dare say," smiling and shaking his head at her.

"Well, then, the upshot of what I mean is, that two people like you and me have a better right to talk together than a woman has to come into a house because it happens to be her own."

She puzzled a little over this, as if not quite catching his meaning, then she looked at him. How handsome he was, and how much more than handsome; such a distinguished air—such refinement and ease in every movement and gesture; a self-contained man, who was—what he was—independent of others, because he was really himself. What an irresistible attraction she found in his careless, almost scornful grace—in the light that shone in his eyes, and the smile that played about his mouth; a man who was one thing, till he spoke to *her*, and then became another. Had she really some power over him that others had not, and was that what he meant? What a delightful thing friendship was? But was it really possible that he and she were to be friends?

"You and me?" she repeated, doubtfully; "that is to say, Mr. Gregory and—Miss Style?"

Now it was his turn to look a little puzzled, especially at the soft, anxious expression in her lovely eyes.

"No, no," he cried earnestly, trying to follow her thoughts, and watching her as he spoke—"not Mr. or Miss anything, but just the souls and bodies that make *us*, whatever our stations in life or arbitrary names may be."

"Ah!" she said, with a little happy sigh, "but that would be true friendship."

"As true as steel," he cried, his face in a glow.

"And in such a little time," she said, looking quite appealingly at him."

"Oh, don't fall into that mistake—that conventionalism," he cried; "it is quite, *quite* unworthy of you. Some people we know in five minutes, and love in five minutes; and others we could never know and never love, not in five years, or in fifty-five years, or five hundred years."

"That is quite true," she replied, with the sweetest smile of acquiescence. "I have often felt that, in little ways before about people, but never like this—never half so much as now."

His heart beat fast as he heard her words, and the color rushed to his face, but he restrained himself, and scarcely dared let himself breathe, in his anxiety to hide the delight they gave him. In her perfect unconsciousness, her innocence, and her simplicity, he felt, lay his best chance; to disturb that too soon, was to throw down the foundations on which he trusted to erect his castle, before he had a hope of putting others in their place.

"Do you know," he said, after a little pause, in a calm, sorrowful voice, "that I have had very few friends in my life?"

"Really!" she answered, surprised. "But that must have been your own doing, I suppose; I could fancy you care for very few people."

"I did not begin life so," he cried, eagerly; "do any of us? I had my hopes, loves, enthusiasms, but I was unfortunate; in some things I was more unfortunate than most of us are; my father—never— *liked* me."

"Your father—your own father?" she exclaimed, in unbelieving tones.

"My own father," he answered, quietly; "he was not a—*good*—man."

"Oh! how I pity you!" she cried, her soft eyes filling with tears, and looking at him as if she would have done anything to comfort him; "and mine was the best man in the world! Oh! what could one do under such a sorrow, you poor boy!" Her mind had gone into the past, and she was vividly imagining him a boy with a bad father. "What *did* you do?"

He was thinking more of her than of himself. Her delicious pity would have comforted him under a worse affliction than the one which, perhaps, he had never before alluded to, to any living creature.

"I ran away," he replied, after feasting for a few happy, silent seconds on her sweet compassion.

"You ran away!" she cried, charmed with the idea, and thinking to herself—"What a hero you are;" and her eyes expressed the thought plainly enough through their long lashes, though her tongue did not speak.

"Yes," he said, with a far-away look in *his* eyes. "What ages ago it seems! Will the next eighteen years contain a whole life, I wonder? How strange it is to me to think that *I* was that suffering boy! Eighteen years hence, shall I look back on the man I am now with the same strange sensation of another self?"

"Eighteen years hence!" cried Miranda. "Why, I shall be nearly forty!"

Whereat they both laughed, and I cannot say I wonder at them. The idea of its being possible that that lovely impersonation of youth should ever be nearly forty did seem supremely ridiculous.

But Miranda felt as if she was horribly unfeeling to laugh at such a moment.

"You ran away," she repeated. "Oh! why did you do it? and where did you run to?"

"I could not stay in the house," he replied, "I cannot tell you why. I loved my dead mother. Do you know, I think she was a little like you?"

"Like me!"

"At any rate, there is a picture of her hanging in the great saloon—taken when she was a girl, before she married—that has a look of you; it is the loveliest picture I ever saw—you know I never saw a picture of *you*. How I have worshipped it when I was a lad. Poor young mother! she died too soon."

"Oh! I am so sorry," cried Miranda.

"She brought me up well. I wish I remembered better all her good teaching, for then I should be fitter for—"

"For what?"

"Never mind—for what I hope some day to attain. Ask me a week hence, and I will tell you —I hope I will tell you a week hence."

"I shall certainly ask you."

"Do, do; and I hope I shall certainly tell you. Do you think there is anything in the world I should like better than to tell you now? only I don't dare."

"I can't think what you mean," replied Miranda.

"But may I tell you a little about my past life?" said he; "I wish you to know it. The house was full of wickedness, and I felt my dead mother's memory insulted; I felt *that*, though I was such a boy—I am glad I did; and I was miserable, and I couldn't bear it. Men can bear misery, boys can't."

"Oh! it is so sad to be miserable," sighed Miranda.

I suppose it was a very foolish remark, but it sounded to him like the wisdom of an angel.

"And so I set off in the middle of a summer night, and walked a couple of hundred miles, I daresay—day and night, night and day; getting a meal when or where I could, sleeping under a hedge or on a door-step. Heigh-ho! how long ago it all seems!"

"Well?" she cried, breathless.

"Well, at last I reached a place in Wales, belonging to my aunt Gregory, for I thought she might take me in."

"Lady Gregory!"

"Yes, no less a person than Lady Gregory, in whose ballroom we first met. What a figure I was? what a state I was in! David Copperfield was nothing to me when he appeared before Betsey Trotwood. I have read that meeting, with thrills that testified to its reality."

"Oh! go on."

"I felt ashamed to present myself, and so I crept into a barn, and, wrapped up in some straw, fell asleep, if sleep such a stupor of fatigue could be called. Then I was found next morning, more dead than alive, and carried into the house, for I could not stand; and I believe my mind was all astray for a time."

"Oh! poor little boy! how I should like to have comforted you," sighed Miranda, with tears on her cheeks.

"*You*, my darling!—forgive me, I *beg* your pardon; the word came of itself, I couldn't help it; the idea of being comforted by you did seem so sweet. But you were hardly born then; when I was twelve years old, what a dear little toddling thing of two or three you must have been!"

Miranda could not help comparing the graceful

ease, the tender, penetrating glance with which he apologized for his involuntary freedom, with Mr. Gaunt's "Beg pardon, I'm perfectly respectful." Can the two men be of the same race? she asked herself—both so good and so kind (what proofs had she had, I wonder, of the goodness and kindness of Lady Gregory's nephew?), and yet one as superior to the other as light to darkness. So thought Miranda, weighing, as she did, the two men in scales of her own manufacturing. Perhaps if she had then been "nearly forty" she might have judged differently. Perhaps she will judge men differently when she is, perhaps not.

"And what happened?" she asked. "Who did comfort you? poor boy! poor child! I hope some one did."

"A little girl, who was staying with my aunt, happened to run into the barn to play. She had a dog with her, that, routing about among the straw, came suddenly upon my feet sticking out in a corner, and barking loudly, drew her attention to them. I was covered with the straw in which I had rolled myself, but my feet, as I said, stuck out. She seized hold of them, and began pulling them violently."

"Oh!" cried compassionate Miranda, who, while

she listened, actually trembled with sorrowful interest.

"I groaned, for my feet were all blistered and sore, and the anguish was really too much. She found her hands covered with blood, and rushed, roaring, from the barn, telling everybody that there were two wicked dead feet in a barn, groaning, and somebody had been murdered, all but his feet! I remember this way of telling what she had seen became a standing joke against her afterwards."

"She must have been a very disagreeable little girl, I think," said Miranda.

"She is a very disagreeable woman now," he replied, composedly; "it was Miss Hitchcock."

"Oh dear!" said Miranda, "how very, very odd!"

"But now," said he, "that I have told you some of my history, does it make you pity me a little? do you feel a little kindly towards me?"

"Oh!" she cried, "as if that was necessary. But I do, indeed I do; I never heard anything more interesting."

It requires very little to interest a girl of eighteen when it is told to her by a handsome man of eight-and-twenty.

"And will it really make you think of me now and then?"

"Of course I shall think of you?"

"I'm not fond of talking about myself—generally I hate it—but to-day, do you know, it gives me exquisite pleasure."

"There is nothing in the world I like so much as when a friend talks to me about himself."

"Do you really? how kind of you. I think you are the kindest person I ever met."

"But I hope *they* were kind to you—your aunt Gregory, did she take care of you then?"

"Yes; that was how I was so much thrown into her— However, I went to school, and after that to college. I was about two-and-twenty when my father died."

"He is dead! Ah!"

She was thinking of his not being good. She longed to ask if he had repented, but felt that the subject was too sacred to be handled by her.

"I have something more I wish to tell you," continued he. "I found my property deeply in debt; and I was surrounded by advisers as to how I might avoid paying the debts; but, though not legally bound, I considered that I was bound in honor, and so by careful economy, in the course of some years, I paid them all."

"How noble," thought Miranda, enchanted. "It is just like the hero of a novel!"

"It was very good of you to pay them," she said, softly and a little timidly.

"No, no," he cried hastily, and coloring; "it's not for that I told you. An honorable man couldn't do otherwise. It's only that I want you to know something about my life—to understand the trials that I have had, for then you will make allowances for me—it is not that I am praising myself."

"Oh! I *know* that," she cried, eagerly; "pray don't suppose for a moment that I thought otherwise."

"A thousand thanks," he replied. "I believe you understand me better than anybody ever did before, and I am telling you more of what I felt than I have ever told to living soul; and I will admit, then, that it was a hard time while the debts were being paid. Men did not enter into it, and it placed me at a disadvantage with my contemporaries; it was then that I drew back from many friendships, and, thrown on the society of women—most affectionately treated by my aunt Gregory and her intimates—it was then that the great mistake of my life was made."

The meaning, obscure as it was, in this last sentence, Miranda did not take in at all. She heard the words, it is true, and they may recur to her some future day when circumstances have given them a meaning, but her mind was at this moment so full of his noble life, that it failed to remark there had been a mistake in it.

"Yes, I do understand," she said, timidly; "it must have been very hard."

"It *was* hard," he said. "There were things connected with that time of self-denial I don't like to think of now; but I wish *you* to think of me sometimes, and I am so glad you should know just a little about my life. You *will* think of me sometimes, will you not?"

"Indeed I will," said Miranda; and then added, simply, "how can I help it?"

"I have thought of little but you since we first met," continued he, making his voice as expressionless as his glowing thoughts would permit. "It is but fair you should give me a thought now and then."

"Oh! but I—" began she, eagerly; but she

paused, blushing, without completing the sentence. Her innate modesty taught her, without teaching, that even in friendship it was the man's part to *make* it, and the woman's to receive. We never hear of making friendship, and yet it is, perhaps, almost as much an art as making love.

"But you?" he cried. He had been very prudent and cautious hitherto. He felt the extreme shortness of their acquaintance, and was in constant fear of her taking alarm ; but now, for a moment, he slipped out of the restraint he had put on himself, and could not forbear urging her—a kind word or two would be such a sweet gift to carry home with him. "But you— ?" he cried.

Miranda had collected herself, and turned her bright eyes frankly on him.

"But I," she said, gently, "have promised to be your friend, and friends must think of each other."

How he adored the perfect modesty of even her innocent unconsciousness ; how he thanked his fate for having thrown such a woman in his way, and given him such chances of winning her ; how he vowed in his own heart that he *would* win her ; and while she restored to him all the beauty and freshness of his lost youth, his whole life should be devoted to making hers happy. Then a horrible thought flashed across his mind—had she ever cared for anybody else? He looked at her and felt its utter absurdity. That child, with the woman still dormant within her,

"The perfect woman, nobly planned,"

whom his love was to call into life! Still he *knew* the idea, once roused, would haunt him unless it was now laid, so it found utterance in a question.

"Are you such a friend to anyone else?" he said, afraid of his own words as he heard them spoken.

She smiled and shook her head.

"I have only Sophy," she replied, and then a flood of delight came over her face as she thought of the new joy he had given to her life, and he *saw* that the delight was for him.

It took him a moment or two to quiet himself before he could speak again.

"And now," he said, "I have, of course, something more to say. Now I must tell you about"— he stopped—he was unwilling to speak the name— unwilling to plunge into that part of the subject, but he felt it must be done, and so, getting up his courage, he went on—"about Miss Hitchcock."

"About Miss Hitchcock!" cried Miranda, extremely surprised. "Why, what can you have to say—"

But here they were interrupted, and in the most unexpected manner.

CHAPTER VIII.

POOR MISS HITCHCOCK!

WHAT happened was—a great banging of doors, a great scuffling of feet, a great murmur of voices, and several loud screams. The two friends looked at each other for a moment, and then, with one impulse, they both ran out into the lobby. The noises, all different, yet all mingled together in a strange heap, continued; but in the back drawing-room they could only hear—in the lobby they could hear, and they could also see.

What they saw was this—

Something (no, surely it could not be *some one*) being carried up stairs by men, other men following, and a woman here and there screaming.

"What is it?—what can it be?—what is the matter?" cried Miranda, adding to the confusion.

"Hush, hush!" said her companion, gently. "Nothing shall come near you or harm you. Let me go on and see what it is."

A maid-servant was standing at the head of the stairs screaming.

"My mistress, sir!" she cried in reply to his calm inquiries. "Miss Hitchcock, sir! Murder! Fire! Murder! Oh!—oh!—oh!"

And the screams rose louder and shriller than ever.

"It's only a haccident, sir," said the coachman, from below, speaking over the heads of the crowd; "the 'orses took fright—they did—hand a bus drove right into hus, and smashed my poor carridge hall to bits."

"And the lady too," said a man who was helping to carry Miss Hitchcock up stairs. "There's not two bits put right together in her whole body, poor soul!"

"Nonsense, man!" said a policeman; "don't terrify the gentlefolks. The lady's stunned sir, and met with an accident; and there may be some bones broke, no doubt; but I don't *think* she's killed."

"Some of you people, instead of crowding where you're of no use and are not wanted, run off to Dr. Simpkin's, No. 4 Brook Street, and bring him here directly," said Lady Gregory's nephew.

"Now, then, carry her into her own room, and put her on the bed." Then turning to Miranda, he added, with the utmost gentleness, "Had you not better go back into the drawing-room? it is a sad sight, and not fit for you."

Miranda hesitated. She was quite unaccustomed to distressing scenes and sights, and shrank from them with the sensitiveness of youth; but if she was now but a girl, almost a child, she was, as Mr. Gregory (?) had felt, to be a woman one day, and she had all a woman's noblest instincts and capabilities within her.

"Perhaps," she said timidly, "I might be of some use; the servant seems *frightened.*"

She trembled with fear herself as she spoke, but still she walked quite bravely into the room where they were carrying *her,* or *it*—which? Very often our acts are bravest when our spirits are most afraid.

Poor Miss Hitchcock was laid down on her bed, and left there. Miranda and Mr. Gregory (we will call him so, as we know him by no other name) stood beside her—no one else ventured into the room—but a few flurried, whispering people were huddled together outside the door.

The room was a beautiful one—light blue tapestry adorned the bed and the windows; the carpet, covered with roses, felt like moss under your feet;

lace and gilding, gilding and lace, met the eye everywhere ; and there, among it all, lay the brown, ugly, disagreeable-looking woman — her eyes shut, her mouth open, her face swelled, her fists clenched— dead, perhaps, or perhaps just going to die.

"And this is the end of all," said Mr. Gregory. What he meant Miranda did not divine, any more than she understood the remorse in his voice.

She was thinking of being of use—shrinking from the sight of possible death, for the first time, or of the still greater horrors of a possible half recovery —anxious to bring an appearance of life back into that miserable face, though terrified at the idea of what she might see if she succeeded. Under the most favorable circumstances, there is something ghastly in the struggles of the freed spirit, which our own efforts are forcing back into the passive body, incapable of assisting its return.

Miranda found and used salts and scents and water—everything in abundance and ready to her hand —everything except life, which it appeared to her was not to be found.

At last she turned a look of appeal—almost of reproach—on Mr. Gregory, who stood there frowning down at the insensible face.

"She can't be—*dead?*" she cried; and the last word came out with a sound like a little scream.

"No, no," he said. "I think not—I hope not—I trust not—she *can't* be dead."

"There seems no injury—nothing broken—there is no—" She did not finish the sentence, but looked expressively at the fair white coverlet. "It can *only* be her head."

In her ignorance she spoke of mischief to the head as of a less evil than to the limbs.

"I think she is very much hurt," was his only reply.

"Does she live with nobody?" asked Miranda, in a very low voice, as if she was afraid of disturbing her.

"With her father, who is out of town."

"Oh! her poor father!" said she, the ready tears on her eyelashes. "Oh! what will he do!"

"He will bear it very well," replied Mr. Gregory bitterly. "Of course he will be shocked and sorry; but these ties are not always what you think. This father and daughter were not congenial, and were neither of them, I suppose, capable of very strong affections."

"I don't know," replied Miranda, her mind taking

a sudden leap back to a past day ; "she cried at my singing."

I hardly understand why this remark struck him so forcibly. He stared at her with blank eyes ; a wave of feeling passed over his face, leaving it white, and with a scared look in it.

"Cried at *your* singing?" he said, with excitement. "Oh! that would be too much—that would be too much."

I don't believe he himself knew what he meant by this, or why the idea should affect him so powerfully; but at the moment, it seemed to him to be more than he could bear.

At last—what an at last it was to them both—would Mr. Gregory have believed, ten minutes before, that time *could* pass so slowly in Miranda's presence? —at last, then, the doctor arrived. He made his examination, and applied his remedies, and shook his head.

"There is still hope," he said. "I can do nothing more at present ; but there is still hope. She may lie for twenty-four hours in this way, and at any moment she *may* recover her senses. She must be constantly watched. If she comes to herself, I must be sent for immediately, at the moment. If she seems weak, a little brandy should be given; if excited, cloths dipped in vinegar and water should be laid on her head. Those are all the directions for the present, and anyone can carry them out. By-and-by, if she recovers her consciousness, the services of a professional nurse may be required; but her own maid can do all that is wanted now. In fact, I think the only thing wanted is for some one to sit in her room, for I have no idea she will rouse from this stupor for twelve or fourteen hours at the earliest."

Miranda turned and called in the maid, who, when she found what was required of her, flatly refused to do it. She declared she had never been engaged for that sort of work; it had never been put into any of her characters; she had been warned years ago that she ought never to be frightened; she never could be bold enough to sit by the bedside with *that* on it; she couldn't touch her—no, not she, never—neither to put brandy to her lips nor water on her head; and she had never supposed anything of the sort would ever be evened to her. And so, with a great many more " nevers," she went off into a flood of tears, and evidently thought, that of all the household she was the person to be most pitied. Dr. Simpkin had before this taken his leave, promising to look in again in the evening, if he was not summoned before.

"Very well," Miranda said; "then I will sit with her for the present; the poor thing must not be left in this way. Alas! how lonely some people are!"

"Not when visited by an angel," said Mr. Gregory, in a low voice. "But will you really watch by her?"

"Certainly I will," was the reply; "it would be actual cruelty to do anything else."

"I can't pity her, so guarded; I would almost change places with her if I thought I should open my eyes and find you there. Meantime, I must go. We shall both be employed on the same work, for I must follow her father and break the news to him. You will think of me—won't you?—while you are watching the daughter and I am hurrying after the father. I like to believe that you will think of me."

"Yes, I shall think of you," replied Miranda, softly, and seating herself by the bedside.

He lingered as long as he decently could, but few pretences for such delay offered themselves, and after a minute or two he was obliged to take his leave.

And so Miranda was left behind—a solitary watcher by the senseless body of a woman who might be dead or who might be dying—a stranger to her, of whose very name she was ignorant a few days before.

"And all this—everything that has happened since—all comes of my trying on Miss Hitchcock's wedding dress," thought she.

Then with a great start, as the accustomed words, "Miss Hitchcock's wedding dress," passed through her mind, she remembered that *this* was Miss Hitchcock—this dead or dying creature beside whom she now sat was the very Miss Hitchcock whose wedding dress she had tried on.

She looked round the room, replete with every comfort and luxury that money could procure, and thought of its living mistress moving about in it. A large Psyche glass stood opposite the bed. She imagined Miss Hitchcock standing before this glass, on the morning of her wedding day, trying on the very dress that *she* had made. That is what was to have been; and, instead of that, was the present scene all—that she, the dressmaker, was to watch by the death-bed of the bride? And would the shining satin and delicate lace never be worn, except by her on that night, which now seemed so far away, when she went dancing through the splendid rooms at Lady Gregory's ball? She shuddered and hid her face in her hands, and thought, with a sort of terror, of that beautiful dress in which she had been so happy. Then, naturally enough, the idea of Mr. Cressingham presented itself to her mind—handsome and fashionable and charming as Sissy had described him—not caring for the woman he was marrying for her money, and snubbed by her in return. Where was he now? What would he feel when he heard of this dreadful accident— this life and death struggle in her who ought to be dearer to him than all the world beside, and with whom he had contemplated spending his future life? Would he be sorry? Would he feel remorse that he had not cared for her, and not caring for her, would have married her? Would a late love as well as a late repentance spring into being when it was *too* late, and death had taken for its own, her whom he should have loved in life?

Hours passed away while lost in endless reveries. Miranda held her weary watch in Miss Hitchcock's bedroom. Evening was closing round her, its shades falling early in a London room at the back of the house, looking towards a narrow street. Patiently had the girl sat through all this time, performing the duty of the good Samaritan by a stranger—a duty which she supported calmly while daylight lasted. But with the approach of night, who announced his advent by the voice of the soft summer twilight, a strange restlessness took hold of her. Vainly she attempted to resist it; it was too powerful—its strength was stronger than hers; and unable any longer to sit still, she slowly and reluctantly rose to her feet. The great Psyche mirror had an irresistible attraction for her. She knew not why, but she felt as if she must approach it and look boldly into its depths, in order to rid herself of the strange meaningless fears that were oppressing her. She had been conjuring up a figure in bridal costume standing before that mirror to see itself reflected in the bright crystal, till the idea haunted her that a ghostly bride must be there— there *in* the glass—and that if she looked at the shining surface, she should see this ghostly bride instead of herself. She felt she could only lose the horrid fancy by seeing herself really reflected in the mirror, and then a sort of hurry seized her to do so at once. " It will soon be dark, it will soon be dark," she kept saying to herself, " and I shall never, never know; and suppose the fancy should not leave me, and I should all my life be haunted by the knowledge of that ghostly bride shut up in the looking-glass!" She knew how foolish she was, and yet she could not help it. She did not really believe in the notion, and yet, acting as if she did, in another moment she had glided forward and placed herself in front of the hanging glass.

She saw no brown, ugly woman in bridal finery there—no satin robe, its rich folds sweeping the ground, softened by the light draperies of exquisite lace—only a slight young figure, in simplest dress, and a fair, pale face crowned by a wealth of chestnut hair. There seemed to Miranda, however, a new expression in that face which she had never seen in it before; when had it come, and what was it? She could not tell, but somehow it looked to her less childlike—more thoughtful than its wont; what was it? She was puzzled, startled— she gazed earnestly at it, and the expression died away; had it been as if a soul was just passing into life? She saw the bed behind her in the glass, and suddenly a head rose up from the pillow, a ghastly, brown face appeared, and two great eyes stared helplessly and beseechingly at her. In terror, the wildest and the most unreasonable she had ever experienced in her life, she turned desperately round to discover that Miss Hitchcock was alive.

Another moment brought her to the bedside, looking anxiously into her face to determine what the treatment was that ought to be pursued; but first she rang the bell twice, the signal that it had been agreed she should make if the doctor was to be sent for.

"Am I ill?" said Miss Hitchcock.

"I think you are better," replied Miranda, gently.

"Where is Arthur?"

Miranda hesitated an instant, and then answered—

"Do you wish me to send for him? I dare say he would come. Where does he live?"

"Better not; better not; it is too late—too late. I won't do what he asks me; and I will be rich, and I will live as I like. Too late—too late—too late."

Then Miranda got frightened, and placed a handkerchief saturated with vinegar and water on her forehead. She muttered incoherently to herself, and suddenly closing her eyes again, became quite quiet.

She had spoken in a weird, wild way—quite unlike Sophy's wanderings when she called for George. Oh! poor Sophy. How intensely, as the thought of Sophy flashed across her mind, did Miranda feel that she loved her. This was a delirium, if delirium it was to be called, in which she could imagine the spirit, that had broken free from the restraints of the body, saying *wicked* things. The manner in which the woman's lips moved to utter words that those lips had lost the power to restrain, appeared very dreadful to Miranda. She shrank from the unconscious creature who had declared so vehemently that she would be always rich and do as she liked, while the constantly repeated "too late" sounded in her ears like the wail of a lost soul.

She breathed more freely when silence reigned again in the room, and she sent up an earnest prayer to God for the poor pitiable girl in the bed; for suddenly the idea of Miss Hitchcock's *youth* appealed to Miranda's heart with all the force of a new and most pathetic discovery.

So plain, so dark, and so independent, it had

never occurred to her before that she was *young;* but now she recognized the fact for the first time, and a flood of pity and sorrow came over her as she did so.

"Poor thing! poor thing! poor, *poor* thing!" she kept saying to herself; and the kind, gentle thoughts, the tender hopes, the earnest wishes—every one of which, if not a prayer in form, was a prayer in fact—that rose from Miranda's heart and floated over the bed, must surely, in their innocent strength, have wrought *some* good, either here or hereafter, for the far different spirit in whose behalf they were framed.

Just then came a little tap at the door, and Miranda, flying to open it, found a small page, all silver lace and buttons, standing outside.

"Is it the doctor?" cried she, breathless.

"Yes-miss," answered the smart boy smartly; and at the same time a gentleman came up stairs.

She advanced a step to meet him, and, to her extreme astonishment, found herself face to face, not with Dr. Simpkin, but with Mr. Gaunt.

"Mr. Gaunt!" cried she, all amazement.

"To be sure," was the reply, in his bluff, hearty tones; "why not? The women were getting bothered at your staying so late; Miss Sophy told me where you were hanging out, and so here I am."

"Oh! I am so glad," she said; "you can tell Sophy I can't help staying late. The lady has met with an accident. She has no one to sit with her, and I am doing so just for the present."

"Hullo!" said he; "turned sick nurse. That's a new trade, isn't it?"

"But I am so surprised Dr. Simpkin doesn't come."

"Please, miss," said the smart boy, "Dr. Simpkin's been and gone, and been sent for to one of the Princesses; and I thought this was t'other doctor, come in *his* place, when *he* said he wanted *you*."

A thundering knock at the hall door, and the smart boy winked at himself, as one who would say, "Here he is; that's your ticket!" and disappeared down the stairs.

"Much harm done?" asked Mr. Gaunt. "What sort of accident? Any bones smashed?"

"The injury seems almost entirely to the head," replied Miranda.

She had stationed herself in such a position by the partially open door, that she commanded a view of the bed, and so would be instantly aware of any movement on Miss Hitchcock's part.

"Do you like watching and nursing?" asked Mr. Gaunt, looking at her curiously. Perhaps his artist-eye had become conscious of new capabilities in her Miranda face.

"No," she replied, frankly, "I don't; it frightens me; but I like being of use. I wonder whether another doctor has come instead of that one?"

But instead of a doctor, a girl, in fashionable promenade costume, came running up stairs.

"We've only just heard," she said; "we're so shocked. Is she killed?—is she hurt? What is it?"

After one puzzled moment, Miranda recognized Miss Maria Leslie.

"She is not killed," she replied, "but she is very much hurt."

"What an awful shame!" said Maria.

Mr. Gaunt regarded the pretty, fragile creature with admiration, and said, half-aloud, "Hullo, *Ariel!*"

Miss Leslie, in her turn, looked at him with open-eyed interest.

"What is it?" asked she of Miranda, very much as if she was being shown a new wild beast.

"Mr. Gaunt," said Miranda, "Miss Leslie."

But Maria's attention was now concentrated on Miranda herself.

"Good gracious!" cried she, "is it really *you?*—my soprano! How awfully jolly!"

"I suppose I've no business here," said Mr. Gaunt, gruffly. "Very well; shall I take your message to Miss Sophy? When will you come home yourself?"

"I don't know," said she, rather perplexed; "I have hardly thought of anything. I must stay here while I'm wanted, mustn't I?"

He looked at her with a sort of half-savage kindliness, and said—

"Good girl!"

Miss Leslie edged up to Miranda, and with a side glance at Mr. Gaunt, whispered—"Does it bite?"

"Too late!—too late!—too late!" wailed the voice from the bed within.

Miranda turned, like a traitor who has been detected in having left his post, and hastily retreated through the door.

"How awfully horrid!" cried Maria, quite pale. "Oh! what shall I do?"

"Be of use, like her," growled Mr. Gaunt, jerking his thumb in the direction that Miranda had taken.

"Oh, no! I can't," said Maria, pitifully; "I never was of any use in my life."

"Too late!—too late!" said the voice.

"Oh! don't, you horrid!" cried Maria, and began to cry.

But Mr. Gaunt strode into the room, put Miranda on one side, usurped her place by the patient, covered her forehead with the saturated handkerchiefs, and bustling about among the bottles on the table, found something that he poured down her throat.

Then he said to Miranda, in a low voice, "This is no place for you, and I sha'n't leave you here; I shall fetch a nurse and a doctor, and then I shall take you home."

"Thank you," replied Miranda, from her heart.

Mr. Gaunt then strode out again to Maria, who was crying in the lobby.

"Haven't you got a thingamy here?" asked he.

"A what?"

"A thingamy! are you deaf? A—a coach and four, of course, I mean—a carriage of some sort?"

"Yes; I am driving, certainly."

"Well, may I take it a minute, and bring a nurse and doctor?"

" Oh no, no ; I daren't stay here. I should die of fright ; I should indeed ! "

" Then come with me ; you don't look bad, and you wouldn't like your fiddle-faddles to stand in the way of saving a life, I'm sure."

She gave him a quick glance.

" Yes, I will," she said ; " you don't look bad either."

And so this strangely-matched pair drove off together in Miss Leslie's well-appointed carriage.

Miss Hitchcock remained perfectly quiet during their absence, which appeared to Miranda intolerably long, though in reality the time Mr. Gaunt took to perform *any* business was about half that occupied by the generality of mortals for the same purpose.

At last he appeared, bringing with him, as he had promised, a doctor and a nurse. The former could do no more than repeat the opinion and the directions given by Dr. Simpkin ; but the latter was most welcome to Miranda, her presence restoring to her a liberty which had been so strangely taken from her.

" It seems to me all like a dream," she said, as she walked slowly home with Mr. Gaunt.

" A bad dream ? " suggested he.

"Oh no, no!" she cried quickly, and her thoughts flew back to her conversation with Mr. Gregory. "A wonderful dream, a strange dream—things leading one into another, as they only do in dreams—but *not* a bad dream."

"You look as if you had gone to sleep in one world and woke up in another," said he, in what sounded like a tone of complaint.

"Do I?" she replied, softly. "I *did* live in a new world all the time I dreamt, and I feel as if I was in it still—I can't realize that I am going home to Sophy and her garret. Oh, my dear Sophy!"

"Yes; that's *it*," growled he; "you have been in a grand house and a beautiful bedroom—all filigree and fleur de lys, hang them—and you can't understand going home to a garret. That's *it!*"

"Is that all you know about it?" cried she. "Do you *really* think that's *it?*" and she laughed her innocent, gay girl-laugh, which sounded for the first moment almost strange in her own ears.

However, something either in the laugh or in herself contented Mr. Gaunt, for he looked at her quite kindly, and repeated over again what he had said before—

"Good girl."

It was the sweetest happiness to Miranda to find Sophy so much better. A tender embrace and heaps of kisses made up for the long absence, and then Miranda, seated by her sister's side, told her the whole history of the afternoon's events—beginning with Mr. Gregory and ending with poor Miss Hitchcock.

CHAPTER IX.

EXPLANATIONS.

"BUT," said Sophy, with a bewildered face, "who is he?"

"Oh, Sissy!" how can you ask? It is Mr. Gregory—Lady Gregory's nephew, of course. Did I really only call him *he*? But even so, who else *could* it be?"

"You called him Mr. Gregory; it's not that, but who is he? where did you meet him? how are you friends?"

"Oh, Sissy, Sissy! you *can't* have forgotten him— it's the one I danced with at Lady Gregory's ball."

"At Lady Gregory's ball!"

"Oh, Sissy, Sissy, Sissy! what *can* you mean?"

"Oh, Miranda! what can *you* mean, I think it is; I have not the least notion what you are talking about. The one you danced with at Lady Gregory's ball? But you don't know any Lady Gregory, and never went to a ball in your life."

"Oh! how can you say so, when I told you all about it—the ball I went to in Miss Hitchcock's wedding dress."

"In Miss Hitchcock's wedding dress! Please don't, Miranda; I'm not strong, and you tire and worry me—it *is* such nonsense, and you say it all with such a grave face; please don't."

"But I must, Sissy. I'm very sorry, only I must; it's all true, every word of it, and I told you all about it when you were ill. Is it really possible you have forgotten it all?"

"You never told me a word," replied Sophy, with energy.

"Oh! indeed, *indeed* I did! Don't say so; the very first day you were well enough, I told you the whole story."

"Then I must have been too ill to take it in, for I have not the most vague recollection of anything you are talking about."

"Never mind, then; I'll tell it you all over again."

"I'm very sorry," said Sophy, apologetically.

"You needn't be sorry," replied Miranda, her eyes dancing; "there's *nothing* I like so well as telling it—I'm quite charmed that I've got to tell it to you again. Now listen, and be astonished."

Sophy *did* listen; and Sophy *was* astonished. Miranda's daring, and the delightful evening that she had spent in consequence, sounded to her like a fairy tale. She made her repeat over and over again that she had really put on the dress, and really gone to the ball in it, and really passed as one of the guests and not been found out, before she could either believe or understand what she heard; then she scolded a little, and lamented a little, and said it was very wrong and very foolish, and couldn't end well, and must lead to something bad. But when Miranda had brought her story down to its present conclusion, a bright hope, a wild dream, sprang up in Sophy's soft unworldly heart. She looked at Miranda, and felt, rather than saw, how lovely, how sweet, how good she was—a girl to enchant any man—a creature worthy of any rank—that might make any home happy; and so Sophy sank down among her pillows and closed her eyes, and gave herself up to the bewildering prospect that seemed opening before her, and built the most beautiful of all air castles—that which is to contain the happiness of another.

With her true woman's heart, she did not give the girl one hint of all this. She would not have disturbed her unconscious simplicity—no, not even if, by so doing, she could have secured her the lot which she almost believed was within her reach ; nor with her own early dreams safe in her heart, would Sophy for worlds have deprived Miranda of the joy of being.first wakened to love by the lover himself. No sacrilegious hand should shake the bloom from the blossom, which ought to be gathered in all its sweet freshness, if it is gathered at all.

She did not think it prudent to dwell too much on Mr. Gregory to Miranda, and when the first overwhelming feelings were past, and she was beginning to accustom herself to those new ideas and new hopes which had so suddenly invaded their lives, she encouraged her to talk more of her watch in Miss Hitchcock's room, and the possibility of her having to sing at Miss Leslie's charade party, than of her conversations with Lady Gregory's nephew.

Then, after a time, when all these more interesting and exciting subjects had been discussed, Miranda began to remember Mr. Gaunt and his picture, and how he had attended Sophy, and fetched her from Miss Hitchcock's, and how kind and good-natured he had been.

"What a true friend!" said Sophy, when she had heard this almost-forgotten part of the story.

But Miranda had a different idea of true friendship just at that moment, and laughed a little laugh of happy scorn.

"Well, he is very good-natured," said she; "but you can't think, Sissy, how pretty he's made me in the picture. Oh! it *is* nice to be pretty, Sissy; isn't it?"

"Yes, indeed, it is!" replied Sophy, with a smile for the pretty, innocent face that asked the question quite as appealingly as the words did, and a sigh for the days when she too felt the sweet joy of beauty.

"I don't suppose it could have been very naughty of me, after all, to wear Miss Hitchcock's wedding dress," said Miranda, "because I was so heavenly happy, and one *can't* be really happy when one is doing wrong."

"Oh yes, one can," said Sophy; "wrong pleasures make us happy for the time, and *there's* the great danger; papa said so."

"It's not true," interrupted Miranda, before the last three words were out of Sophy's lips, and then stopped in horror at herself. "Oh! of course, I don't mean that; if papa says so it *must* be true, only I don't think it's so with *me*. I dare say it's my fault that it isn't, or that I'm not sensible enough, or something ; but I *do* think I'm never really happy when I'm doing wrong. I do indeed, Sophy."

"Well, you are an innocent sort of a child, Miranda," said Sophy, smiling fondly at her; "so perhaps you are not."

For which speech, gay, loving Miranda kissed her, Sissy half-a-dozen times.

"And now," said poor Sophy, "you must give me some work and take some yourself, for I am afraid, with all these balls and friendships and illnesses, we shall find the purse has been getting empty."

So the two sisters were very industrious that day and the next. Sophy was not strong enough to leave her bed or to work hard, but she sewed on lace and trimmings, and did the easy parts, and, Miranda sang to her all the time. I do believe though they were so poor, and one of them was ill, and they had to labor thus even for their daily food, that at this time both were happy.

In the afternoon Miranda asked rather timidly whether Sophy did not think she ought to go and inquire how poor Miss Hitchcock was.

"I wish it very much," she said, wistfully; "but I also really think I ought."

"I think so too," replied Sophy.

Then Miranda, in her delight at that, performed a little impromptu waltz round the room.

"That was how we did it, Sophy," she cried; "it was thus we went—whirl, whirl, whirl—Mr. Gregory and I. Oh! the delight of dancing; Oh, how sweet, how sweet it is!"

"Look in that press, pet," said Sophy, "and you will find the Indian shawl and some real old lace; with my black silk skirt and your nice little bonnet you will look quite well dressed. Oh! Miranda, perhaps some day—" But here the prudent Sophy broke off; she bit her lip, and with pain and difficulty kept down the words; but the vision of sweet Miranda, splendidly dressed, stepping into her own pretty carriage, suddenly sprang up before her eyes and filled them with tears. Poor eyes, well used to weeping, how strange the tears of happiness seemed to them!

Seldom had any commands of Sophy's been more agreeable to Miranda than these, and with innocent joy she took out the old carefully-kept finery, and attired herself in it; then she went sweeping and careering about the room, twisting herself in all manner of ways, and assuming all the airs of a fashionable lady.

"Shall I do?" cried she; "am I nice? am I pretty? do I look like one of them?" Here she performed a magnificent curtsey. "Oh! there is such a love of a glass in Miss Hitchcock's bedroom, reaching down to the ground, and up and up, ever so much taller than I am; if I had it, Sissy, I should be dancing before it all day; I should indeed. And *isn't* it a pity she's so plain, poor thing! she *can't* take any pleasure in it, *can* she?"

"Perhaps you may have one some day, Miranda."

"I? Oh, Sissy!" and she laughed quite out at the idea of such an impossibility; "as if I should ever save up money, or go without dinners, for *that!* I don't really care about it in that sort of a way, you know—of course I don't; but there's nothing seems to me harder than some people being so very, very plain, and others so very, very pretty." Then she blushed a little, as if afraid she had said a vain thing, and added hastily, "There's Maria, now"—she always thought of Miss Leslie as Maria, and jestingly called her so—"she would like to dance all day before that glass; and poor

Miss Hitchcock, why, if she only danced there just one little minute, it would be enough to make her cry with vexation at seeing what she was like."

And the idea of Miss Hitchcock dancing at all in front of the mirror was so grotesque and incongruous that she was obliged to stop to laugh, Then she suddenly became grave.

"That comes," she said, "of thinking too much of appearance, just as papa used to say; I find it makes me *frivolous*, but I don't *much* mind that; but when it makes me laugh at a poor thing for being ugly, oh, that *must* be very wrong indeed. What a pity it is, Sissy, that when we don't mean harm, we can't keep all our thoughts and feelings quite right, and quite *quite* kind."

Miranda became so sorrowful here, that Sophy had to comfort her.

"I really am as vexed as possible that poor Miss Hitchcock is not pretty," Miranda admitted, in her own defence; "and I only laughed because I couldn't help it. I began by really pitying her because she couldn't dance before that glass and feel glad, and then the idea of her doing it made me laugh; but it shows how careful we ought to be about our fellow-creatures; and I will be careful, Sissy, indeed I will."

And so our Miranda kissed Sophy, and went on her way consoled.

As she tripped down stairs, she perceived that the front drawing-room door was ajar. She could not resist just pushing it open and displaying herself for one brief passing second to the astonished eyes of Mr. Gaunt, who was sitting at his table, opposite to it, devouring his early dinner of cold boiled beef, with plenty of pickles and vinegar. There she stood in the doorway like a picture in a frame, only no picture could ever be so fresh, so radiant, or so gay.

"Am I nice?" she cried, and dropped a little curtsey. Then, shocked at her own forwardness, and closing the door with a great bang, she ran laughing down into the hall, and so danced out of the house door, and with difficulty restrained her steps into a proper walk when she found herself in the street.

At Miss Hitchcock's she seemed to be expected, for the smart boy in silver lace and buttons showed her at once into a small, but pretty sitting-room on the ground floor, saying he believed Miss Hitchcock was better and had spoken conscious, but he would make inquiries.

A pompous, very ill-natured looking, middle-aged man shortly afterwards entered the room. He addressed Miranda with great politeness. Regarding her all the time with the most ill-natured expression possible, he overwhelmed her with thanks.

"I really don't know how to thank you enough for your kindness to my poor daughter; it was really too much; such goodness to a stranger could never have been expected. I really don't know how to thank you enough."

And all the time he spoke, he kept looking at her as if he could have killed her.

She smiled and blushed, and said, "Oh! I did nothing. I am glad I was here. But how is she to-day? is she better?"

He shrugged his shoulders.

"She is better after a fashion. She is quiet, and the doctor says she is going on well, but it is to be a most tedious business, and the inconvenience is much to be deplored. I must go out of town. I am greatly to be pitied."

Miranda looked at him in amazement. "You!" she said; and that was all her reply.

"Yes," replied he, not one whit abashed. "You can form no idea. An illness of this kind is a most melancholy thing; you have no notion of the difference it makes in a house. I can't stand it—I can't stand it—no one could. And our bedrooms, most unfortunately, happen to be on the same floor. I always *did* have a feeling, a strong feeling, that she might just as well have gone up another flight of stairs; but then, as mistress of the house— However, it was very thoughtless, when they brought her in, that they did not carry her up at once to her maid's room, instead of taking her into her own— very thoughtless indeed; but some people have no thought. I never can understand people being so inconsiderate to others. It is most inconvenient. I shall have to go out of town. I am really very much to be pitied."

And now he looked at Miranda, quite as if he considered that *she* was to blame, not only for this, but for all the other bad and selfish arrangements made in the world, and as if he would have gladly taken vengeance on her for them all, there and then.

She, in return, felt nothing but disgust for him.

"Does she suffer?" asked she.

"She?—who?—suffer?—what! Hannah?—my

daughter?—Miss Hitchcock? I really am not prepared to answer. I suppose people *must* suffer who meet with accidents; they cannot escape. At present I believe she is generally unconscious; when consciousness returns, it will of course make the case very much more trying, and it would be impossible for me to be in the house. Nothing can be more inconvenient, and I am greatly to be pitied."

"I think poor Miss Hitchcock is fifty times more to be pitied than you are," replied indignant Miranda, with unusual abruptness for her.

"What! Hannah?" cried her father, infinitely astonished.

"And her name is *Hannah* too!" thought compassionate Miranda. "Hannah! such a name to be added to all the rest. She *is* unfortunate."

But she said nothing more; only looked at him with lovely offended eyes, whilst he returned the gaze with that ill-natured expression of his, which may have really meant nothing, and for which, if so, he deserved pity more than his daughter did for her dangerous illness, or even for the great misfortune of having been christened Hannah.

"I only called to inquire," said Miranda at last,

finding the interview extremely unpleasant. "I am so glad she is going on well. Good-morning."

"Oh! but I beg your pardon. I have a message for you, a note; no, a card." Miranda felt her happy heart beating fast, and the rose-blushes rising into her face, as she thought of Mr. Gregory. "I promised to deliver it myself. I placed it here, in my waistcoat pocket, that it might be near the region of the heart, as I told the giver." Here he smiled a most ill-natured smile, and, taking a card from the pocket referred to, presented it to Miranda with a pompous, flourishing bow. She half closed her eyes for half a second, as one anxious to prolong the pleasures of expectation, and then, opening them, they rested on and read the following words. First, printed in the centre of the card, "Miss Leslie;" and secondly, written in pencil below the name, "Do come to me the minute you can; there's a dear. Always tea and chat at 4 P.M. We *must* settle about the soprano. Life's short; heigho!"

The momentary pang of sharp disappointment was succeeded by a feeling of pleasure. How nice to go to "Maria," and settle about the soprano! What an agreeable way of spending an hour in itself! And then—then—was it not all leading to another interview with Mr. Gregory, who had promised to be at the charade party, if she would undertake the soprano?

"I see," she said; "I must not lose any time. It is four o'clock now, and Miss Leslie is expecting me."

"Present to Miss Leslie the expressions of my unchangeable loyalty and devotion, and assure her that it is only to her I would have spared so charming a companion as yourself," replied Mr. Hitchcock, with another pompous, flourishing bow, and looking more than ever as if he would have liked to kill her.

"Oh, what nonsense!" said Miranda; and so saying, she danced out of the room and the house. "And I've no doubt he's sharpening his knife, ready," said she. "Ugh! the monster. And murder itself is not worse than such nasty selfishness; dear, dear, how horrid it would be to feel like *that!*" And so she walked to the other side of the square —no contemptible distance either—and rang and knocked at Mrs. Leslie's door.

It was opened by a footman in livery, while a jauntily-dressed lady's-maid stood behind and peeped over his shoulder.

"Is it the young lady for Miss Maria?" she asked over the shining epaulette.

"Yes," replied Miranda.

"Come this way, please, ma'am. Miss Leslie will be delighted to see you."

And so she brought Miranda up stairs into a little cosy room on the drawing-room floor, fitted up with every luxury as a young lady's boudoir, but with pictures of hunters and jockeys hanging on the walls and a pair of diminutive boxing-gloves lying on the work table.

Maria was lounging in an easy-chair, looking a little pale and disconsolate.

"Oh!" said she, raising herself languidly up, "is it you? I am glad; but I am so sick;" then she fixed her large soft eyes plaintively on Miranda. "Can you smoke?"

She looked so small, so fragile, and so feminine.

"Smoke!" cried Miranda. "What *do* you mean? Smoke what? How? Glass, or drawings, or what?"

"Pipes," said Maria, laconically.

"Pipes!"

"Yes, of course, not real pipes—those are only for man, lucky man—but cigars, ci—cigarettes; *can* you smoke them?"

There was a world of plaintive anxiety in her voice and face.

"*I* smoke them?" replied the amazed Miranda. *I?* Of course not—I never tried."

Maria sank back among her pillows, turning a little paler still.

"Well, I have," said she, "and I can't, they always make me sick; it *is* so hard, isn't it? and when I really do try my very best."

"But why do you try?" asked Miranda, innocently. "Have you asthma?"

"Asthma!" cried Maria. "No, thank you; I'm not an old fogy, am I? Do I look like asthma? I try it because it's good form, and because I can't *bear* that men should have *all* the pleasures—it is *so* unfair."

"But they haven't, have they? I'm sure I don't think they have. I'm sure we have heaps of pleasures."

"I wonder what they are," sighed Maria. "Here am I as sick as anything—oh! so sick—because I smoked a tiny little cigarette for three minutes; and there's Ned, my brother, you know, smokes fifteen real cigars in the day and *enjoys* it, and I think them horrid, and I can't bear the smell. Oh, how hard it is!"

"Hard that you can't do what you don't like? That is a new sort of hardship, surely."

"No, hard that I can't like what I want to do," replied Maria, rather sharply. "I thought you'd sympathize with me, and perhaps teach me how."

"No, indeed," said Miranda, laughing, and wondering to herself what Mr. Gregory would think of a woman smoking. "If I had found you with the tiniest cigar in your mouth conceivable, I'd have twiched it out of your mouth directly."

"Would you really, now? Oh, I'm afraid you're not at all sound in your ideas, and you so larky; I thought you'd be up to anything."

Miranda laughed and shook her head.

"It's awfully hard lines on girls," said Maria.

"I don't think so one bit," cried Miranda, energetically. "I think a girl's life is delicious."

"I don't see it," replied Maria. "I wish I did. And then girls have to marry, you know."

Miranda blushed.

"Yes," she said, very softly, "sometimes."

"Sometimes!" almost screamed Maria, sitting upright in her chair, and the color coming back into her face from surprise. "Why, it's the one thing they always have to do."

"No, indeed," replied Miranda, "not always; not unless—"

"Unless what?"

"Why, of course you know what I mean—a girl must care for somebody very much—oh! very much indeed—before she consents to leave all she loves for his sake."

Miranda blushed while she spoke, and looked like the sweetest picture of maiden modesty conceivable. I think if Mr. Gaunt had seen her, he would have taken her portrait on the spot, and called it Dawn; for to an experienced eye there surely was the dawn of love to be seen in her fair, innocent face.

"Is that all you know about it?" answered Maria, disdainfully. "Well, I wonder where you were reared."

"I'm sure," said Miranda, "my ideas are more usual than yours."

"How would you like to marry that Hitchcock, then?" asked Maria.

"Marry who?"

"That Hitchcock."

"What Hitchcock?"

"The man who gave you my card—who sent you here."

"What, old Mr. Hitchcock!" cried Miranda, displaying all her pearly teeth in a burst of laughter —" Miss Hitchcock's father?"

"Yes, old Mr. Hitchcock — Miss Hitchcock's father—how would you like to marry him, I say?"

"Why, not at all, of course," laughed Miranda. "What girl would?"

"Here's the girl who's got to do it, then," replied Maria, in a half comic manner, tapping her chest as she spoke.

"Oh, nonsense! How can you say such a thing?"

"I don't say, I *will* do it; but, I've *got* to do it; they all *want* me to do it, and they're always going on at me about it."

"Oh, dear! and is the poor, foolish old man really in love with you? What a pity!"

"He's not offered yet; but they're always telling me it's in my own hands, and that I may thank myself if he doesn't."

"Oh! do take care and keep him back, then. It must be so sad to have to refuse a man, and an old man, too."

"I've refused heaps of men," replied Maria.

"Have you really?" said Miranda, looking at her with mingled pity and respect.

"Yes, I like it; don't you?—it's something to do, and it's a sort of revenge upon them for being men, while we're only women. I do so hate being a woman."

"But *they* can't help it," replied Miranda, gravely.

"I say," said Maria, suddenly, "that beast of yours didn't bite."

"Beast of mine!" repeated Miranda, looking about her in astonishment. "What do you mean? I haven't got a beast."

"Doesn't it belong to you—that wild man of the woods I carried off in my carriage with me? I thought it did. He ordered me about, and took me to a hospital here and a house there; and he filled up my thingamy, as he called it, with nurses and doctors, without 'with your leave,' or 'by your leave;' but he didn't bite. I think he's a very nice beast."

"He is very good-natured."

"Has he got any name? What do they call him? Has Frank Buckland seen him? Does he hang out at the Zoo?"

"His name is Gaunt."

"And what is he, if he's not a beast?"

"He's an artist."

"An artist, and his name Gaunt! Oh you're laughing at me now; you're not going to tell me that that's Gaunt the painter."

"I really don't know; his name's Gaunt, and he paints pictures."

"Was he bred a doctor?"

"Oh yes, that he certainly was, for he told me so; and he cured Sophy, and did poor Miss Hitchcock a great deal of good too."

"Well, I *am* astonished—I never was more astonished in my life. So that was Gaunt the painter; and I had a *tête-à-tête* drive with him. What an honor! I'd no more idea of it—don't you know—I'm wild about art. How glad I am I said he was *a nice* beast!"

CHAPTER X.

THE CHARADE.

AT this moment tea was brought in, and Miss Leslie, forgetting all about her sickness and her cigarette, sprang from her chair to exercise the hospitalities of a little tea-table, which she did gracefully enough. Miranda, having dined but scantily, was charmed at the unwonted luxury of this afternoon meal, and ate cake and brown bread and butter till Maria laughed.

"Go on, do go on; take another slice. It's delightful to see a girl eat like that—near the end of the season, too. I *never can* eat as I wish; I've often made myself ill trying; it's too aggravating to see men eat slice after slice, dish after dish. *Why* should they be able to take in so much more than we do? How I *have* tried to eat like a man!"

Miranda laughed.

"Certainly," said she, "the pleasures you envy

are what I should have never given a thought to—
smoking and eating!"

"And drinking!" cried Maria, with great energy.
"Oh, my dear, to see men drink, and *quite* steady
on their legs afterwards! Now two glasses of wine
and a tumbler of beer are as much as I can stand;
and I'd rather not take *them*, at the same time. It's
shameful injustice—horribly shameful. And then
there's not a bit of harm in a man swearing a little—
just a little, you know—not ugly oaths, but spirited;
and then they stand with their backs to the fire in
the most delightful manner, and they may sit just in
any attitude they like."

Miranda laughed heartily at this catalogue of
grievances.

"Not one of which mighty privileges do I envy
them of a bit;" said she; "and, all together, they can't
outweigh a girl's pleasure in being—nice, and finding
herself—liked."

She hesitated over the two words—nice and liked
—which she finally selected, and blushed brightly
before she had finished her speech.

"Yes, but that's only because we can torment man
by it," replied Maria, "so it's not a *selfish* pleasure.
Now all a man's pleasures are *entirely* selfish; they

concern no other people at all, but just him; and it's selfish pleasures that are so *much* the best," added she, discontentedly.

"I'm quite sure that's not true," said Miranda, nodding her head emphatically.

"But all this time," cried her hostess, with sudden recollections—"all this time we have forgotton the soprano."

"And I can't stay *much* longer; but I'm ready now to do anything you like."

"The charade is Ireland, because, you see, it's so difficult to hit on anything new, and we don't think Ireland has been acted before."

"And how do you do it?"

"First of all, you know, somebody has to be angry—that's *Ire;* so we have that old fellow—who was he? an old fellow who knew something and couldn't bear noise. It wasn't Sir Isaac Newton or Mr. Hudson, was it? No, no, it's somebody who was alive the other day; he made a cabinet pianoforte calculate. I couldn't bear the idea of a piano doing sums while I was playing, so I sold mine and bought a grand instead."

"A very good exchange, I should say."

"Well, but what was the name of the man? I

used to remember it by calling him a cabbage, to be sure! Babbage was the name—all right. Well, he's to be at his table studying, when, all of a sudden, all the London cries and disturbances begin outside, one after another, and he goes on getting more and more and more in a rage all the time, and that's *Ire*, you know, and you're to be one of the sounds, for you're to sing a ballad to a creaky, creaky organ. How will you like that?"

"I think it will be great fun."

"All right; so do I, only I call it awfully jolly, why don't you?—great fun's tame. However, what's his name? oh, Cabbage, Babbage—yes, Babbage— is in such a precious state, he forswears earth, and says the only place worth living in is a ship on the sea; so he goes to sea to be quiet, and soon finds out his mistake, and after a bit he's wrecked— there's no end of a storm, and he's no end of a coward; so he's awfully glad when he finds himself on shore again, and he throws himself down flat on his face and kisses the ground. That's *Land*, you know."

"But the sea part must be difficult to act."

"Not a bit of it—it's all managed with millions of yards of green baize, up and down on rollers for the sea, and the wagonette on them for the ship; only we think the coachman will turn rusty and not let us have the wagonette, so Ned's to make him drink first, and then it's sure to be all square."

"And how do you do Ireland?"

"Oh, that's easy enough—we just have two processions that come tearing by the minute the poor old thing's safe on shore—an orange procession and a green procession, with flags, and tunes, and everything; and they set to work fighting, and kill each other right off; and when there's nothing but heaps of dead men all round him—orange heaps and green heaps—two processions, and both of them dead—poor Babbage finds out that London is the best place after all."

"So that your charade has a moral to it."

"A moral, has it? Oh, I hope not; I hate morals. However, I don't think it's a particularly *good* moral; is it?"

"Well, I don't know that it is, particularly."

"Oh, then, I don't mind. I *did* think of bringing in, just at the end, the two Kilkenny cats who fought till there was nothing left of either but the fluff at the end of their tails, because they really *were* Irish, and it would have given an air of reality to the scene ; but mamma said she would not be among the audience if we had fighting cats. Besides, I don't *quite* see how we could have managed it."

" Nor I either, I'm sure."

" And now, will you practice your song ? or, at any rate, try it through ? I've got the most delicious hand-organ, as creaky as possible, *all* out of tune, and doing every single thing under the sun that it shouldn't do—bless it—and you're to sing to it *perfectly* in tune. Now then."

While she spoke she produced the organ from under the sofa, and tossed a song to Miranda ; and the two girls proceeded to their work as well as they could for laughing—Maria grinding the organ with a will, and Miranda singing, her eyes radiant with joy, as they always were when she sang.

"SINGING ALONG.

" What shall I do with this life of mine,
   Singing along through the lanes and streets !
Singing and sunshine are very fine,
   And a smile on every face one meets.

"Youth is so sweet, and the world so fair,
   Singing along through the lovely land ;
I'd rather dance 'mid the daisies there
   Than in a palace so great and grand.

"I am the monarch of all I see,
    Singing along wheresoe'er I please;
Bird and blossom, river and tree,
    Are all so dear to a heart at ease.

"Youth is so sweet, and a life so blest,
    Singing along 'neath the open skies;
Freely I wander or take my rest
    As sunshine wakens or moonlight dies.

"Singing along, oh! singing along—
    Singing along while the world is fair;
Song and sunshine, sunshine and song—
    Am I not finding them everywhere?"

Just as Miranda finished singing there was a little tap at the door—which was ajar, and was then immediately pushed open—and Lady Gregory's nephew walked in.

"What *you*, Arthur?" cried Maria, jumping up from her organ. "How uncommonly jolly!"

Mr. Gregory, however, had only eyes for Miranda, and it was not till he had shaken hands with her, and *looked* all the delight this meeting gave him, that he found time to extend two fingers to Miss Leslie with a languid how-d'ye-do?

"What *could* bring you here at an hour when you are not usually out of bed?" pursued Maria.

"Nonsense," replied he, annoyed. "I was at

Hitchcock's, and learned I should find *you* here," addressing Miranda in a softened voice, "and so I came."

Miranda could not understand the sort of embarrassment she felt at meeting him in the presence of another person.

"I am afraid I must be going," she said.

"I was fortunate in hearing your song," he replied.

"Oh, you have been eavesdropping, have you?" asked Maria.

"Yes," he replied, coolly. "I have been standing for half-an-hour outside that door listening to every word you both said."

"Hoping to hear us discuss your highness—whose name, however, we did not even mention," said Maria. "What a sell!" and she pointed at him with her dainty little finger, and laughed provokingly.

"Not at all," replied he, gravely. "I should have been very sorry if you had said a word about me. To tell you the truth, Maria, I was disgusted with all I heard—with the coarseness of your ideas, and the vulgar language in which you expressed them. You are really a lady; what *is* the use of pretending you are not?"

Maria colored, tossed her head, and said, "Fudge."

"Fudge isn't argument," said he, coldly.

"No more's scolding," was her reply—neither of them appearing to study correctness of grammar or elegance of language in their several speeches.

"You are a nice little thing naturally," said he, "but you are on the high road to become a very nasty one. I wonder what pleasure you have in it —I do indeed."

Whereupon Maria burst out crying, and saying she wouldn't stay there to be insulted, not if he were fifty times her cousin, rushed out of the room, slamming the door after her with a great bang.

He shrugged his shoulders as he looked in the direction she had taken. "It's a great pity," he said. "She really is a good girl in the main, and she is doing her best to become odious; it is the most hideous of all the hideous fashions of the day, worse a thousand times than chignons and pearl powder."

"Is she your cousin?" asked Miranda, timidly.

"Yes— did you not know it?—and half-a-dozen years ago the dearest little doll, blushing at everything, and almost *too* soft and feminine; and now you see what she is."

"Do they all do it!" asked Miranda.

"All? Who? What do you mean?"

"All fashionable ladies—are they *all* vulgar?"

"No, no! thank heaven, no!" replied he, smiling; "but there is this fashion of being fast and talking slang got among them, and some of the silly girls seem to think it an uncommonly clever thing. There never was a greater mistake than that, for any fool can do it; and if they only knew how it disgusts men!"

"I don't think Maria would mind *that*."

"I beg your pardon; that's all talk—a blind put up to hide the real feelings that are so very much the other way. And then the slang, and the using vulgar words—saying 'drunk' for 'tipsy,' for instance, as Maria did just now, and as I was quite vexed she should do to *you*—there's no wit in it; they fancy it's piquant; and it does provoke a smile, but it's only from the incongruity of such words coming out of such lips, just as the merest approach to a joke that would not meet with a moment's attention in the drawing-room, makes you laugh from the pulpit, not because of its wit, but simply because it is out of place." Mr. Gregory was working himself up into a state of indignation, and quite haranguing

Miranda, who, however, admired all he said extremely, and rejoiced from the very bottom of her innocent heart that she had never, as far as she knew, used a slang phrase in her life. "But oh!" he said, with a sudden change of voice and manner, "don't let us waste our time in talking and thinking of those who are not worthy to be named in the same year with *you*, and into whose faults and errors you would never fall."

"I am afraid," said Miranda, simply and gravely, "that you overrate me very much; I may not have that special fault, but I do assure you I have plenty of faults of my own. Please don't make any mistake about me; it would be *so* unpleasant if you had to change your opinion."

His eyes expressed a little of the love and admiration that these words excited in him; but he only replied, in a very low, restrained voice, "I believe I understand your character better, perhaps, than you do yourself."

"That you easily may," she replied, gayly, "for I never thought about understanding it; I didn't know I had got any particular character at all."

"In that," he answered, in the same low voice, "lies its greatest charm."

"I am quite sure vanity is one of my faults," said she, laughing and blushing. "I find I like being—complimented." She was going to say 'admired,' but some instinct made her change the word to 'complimented.'

"I hope you will like something else," he cried; "something better than all the compliments that ever were paid. I hope you will."

She looked at him frankly, yet a little timidly—smiling, but also with a slight color coming into her cheeks.

"I think I like almost everything," said she.

"Life is very new to you," replied Mr. Gregory, "and as long as life is new everything seems likable."

"But *I* like old things best," said Miranda, with a pretty mutinous expression springing up into her eyes.

"Like what you please," cried he, laughing, "only, among them, like—me."

She nodded her head.

"And yet, not among them either—hardly *among* other things ; I am more aspiring, more presumptuous, than *that;* it is as one apart from others that *I* would be liked."

"As a friend," she said softly, with a bright smile and a brighter blush.

"Yes, he cried, ardently, "as a friend, if only—if only—you understand all that the word may contain."

What more might then have been said who can tell? But Mr. Gregory and Miranda were fated to be interrupted, and always at what was, perhaps, the most interesting part of their conversations. At least so thought Miranda, when just at that minute Miss Leslie re-entered the room. It is possible that at whatever minute she had happened to return Miranda would have thought the same.

"Well," said Maria, "here I am; have you got anything more ill-natured to say to me?" Then glancing at the two whose *tête-à-tête* she had disturbed, and probably making her own observations on them, she added in rather a marked manner, "Pray Arthur, what account did you have of Hannah to-day?"

"And his name is really Arthur," thought Miranda. "How right!—King Arthur—the Duke of Wellington—*the* most beautiful name in the world!"

"Hannah is better to-day," replied Mr. Gregory, quietly and gravely; "the doctor considers that she is going on quite well."

"Out of danger yet?" inquired Maria, sharply.

"I hardly know," replied he, coloring a good deal; "scarcely yet, I should fear. It must be difficult in such a case to pronounce."

"Poor Hannah—poor Miss Hitchcock!" said Maria; "she is greatly to be pitied."

"I don't know any one I pity so much," said Miranda, fervently.

Mr. Gregory looked at her, and Maria asked why?

Miranda hesitated, and at last said she had rather not tell her reasons; but Maria urged her, and "chaffed" her, and tormented her. First she made her say that she had a great many reasons, and then, under pressure, these great many reasons resolved themselves into three. She was then put through a course of questions about the three, and every now and then desired "not to mind Arthur, but to speak up like a man."

"Why should I mind him?" said Miranda. "Well, if you will have it, I'll tell you. I pity her because she—isn't pretty; I pity her because she doesn't look — nice; and I pity her because she — has money!"

"Well, of all the reasons for pitying anybody, that last is the queerest. I'd willingly be an object of compassion on those terms; I would indeed," said Maria. "But, oh! who would have thought it was so late; there's the dressing bell."

"And I must go," said Mr Gregory; then, as he took leave, he said in low, persuasive accents to Miranda, "Will you call at No. — to-morrow about four? Will you?"

"Yes—if I can—yes," replied she, hurriedly. "I shall certainly want to inquire how she is."

"Thank you," was the only answer; and he was gone.

Maria looked keenly at her.

"He is very fond of lecturing other people," said she. "I wonder whether he ever reflects on what sort of road he is travelling himself, or where it will lead him to."

"What *can* you mean?" cried Miranda, indignant at the inference conveyed as much by the manner in which they were spoken as by the words themselves.

"Never mind," replied she; "only slang is a trifle compared with some other peccadillos; and people who live in glass houses shouldn't throw stones."

"That remark cannot apply to your cousin," said Miranda, with extraordinary dignity of manner.

"Oh, can't it? Very well—so much the better for him, then."

Miranda now wished her good-bye, and, notwithstanding this slight tiff, the salutations exchanged between the two girls were cordial in the extreme, nor would Miss Leslie allow her to take her departure till she had promised to return on an early day to practise the song.

Miranda trod on air all the way home, and her one thought was that she should see Mr. Gregory again the next day, about four o'clock; for certainly, she reflected, he never would have asked me so earnestly, and thanked me so warmly, if he had not meant to be there himself. Oh, how good he is!—how noble he is!—how delightful he is! and she stood still for a moment on the pavement, while a flood of glory seemed to overwhelm her, and compass her round about, from the mere thought of him—that there was such a man in the world—that she had met him —and that he had chosen her for his friend.

She ran gayly in to tell Sophy everything. Poor, patient, hard-working Sophy, who had been busily plying her needle through the afternoon hours of Miranda's absence. Poor, kind, sympathizing Sophy, who put down her work to listen, and had a word, and a kiss, and a look ready for every part of the happy narrative, where word, kiss, or look were required! When an unmarried woman, past her first youth, gives warm sympathy to a girl's love story, I think she is the most unselfish of created beings. I do hope there are crowns of love in heaven for such.

"I can't help liking Maria," said Miranda, "though she *is* vulgar. And if you could see her, Sophy; she is the most refined, soft, delicate-looking little thing in the world, and her mouth is like a rosebud or like a tiny, rosy shell; and when these big, ugly, slang words come tripping out of it, I declare you don't know whether to laugh or to cry."

"Mr. Gregory was very severe on her," said Sophy, "but I hope it may be of use to her; she deserved it."

"Oh, he would not have said it if she had not deserved it," said trusting Miranda; "and it was *that* made me first see how wrong it was—it had been amusing me before like something in a book or at the play; and she looks so sweet and delicate all the time, one can't think the same of her words as if she was a coarse-looking, hulking woman. But when he reproved her, I felt it all in a minute. Oh,

Sissy! I should die if he ever spoke to me like that."

" He couldn't, darling," said Sophy, " because you would never do anything to make him."

" Nobody ever scolded me in my life," said Miranda, " and I can't *think* what I should do if they did."

" But," said Sophy, " do you suppose Miss Leslie really is going to marry Mr. Hitchcock?"

" She said ' they ' wanted her to. I can't think who she could mean by ' they.' They must be very horrid creatures, I'm sure. And what *could* they want it for? A man old enough to be her father, and such a very disagreeable man too! He thought of nobody at all but himself, and he was not the least ashamed to say so. He really did not seem one bit aware that he was going on saying heaps of heartless things every time he opened his mouth. And his face was like the ogre in the fairy tale book at which I always screamed when I was a child."

" Well, he can't help *that*," said rational Sophy.

" Oh yes, but he can," cried Miranda; " because it is the expression in his face that is like. *Any*body can help having an ogre's expression; it would be most unfair if they couldn't. Really, Sissy, I never saw such an ill-natured face in my life before. Poor Miss Hitchcock's is nothing to it—nothing at all."

"I hope they won't marry that poor little thing to him."

"But why should they want to do it, Sissy? and who do you think they are?"

"I suppose," said Sophy, almost reluctant to put such ideas before her innocent sister—"I suppose he is what is called a good match—very rich, you know, and that Miss Leslie's parents want her to marry him on that account."

"Oh, how shocking!" said Miranda, quite appalled. "What dreadful wickedness! Let us *hope*, Sissy, it's not anything so bad as *that*."

Mrs. Green tapped at the door now, and, being asked to enter, gave Mr. Gaunt's compliments, and would the two ladies mind stepping down into his room for half-an-hour, while he just gave a touch or two more to his sketch of Miss Miranda? Sophy was up and dressed that day for the first time, though she had not ventured out of her garret yet; but she thought the change of air and scene would be rather pleasant; so taking Miranda's arm, the two descended the stairs and paid a visit to the first floor.

He received them with bluff cordiality, set chairs for them, and declared himself delighted to see Miss Maxwell " on her legs again."

"You had a close shave," said he;"but it doesn't matter how close when the razor's shut up out of sight in its case again."

Then he took a sheet of paper out of a portfolio, and silently laid it before Miranda, who after looking at it, cried out, astonished, " Maria ! "

For it was a charming little sketch of Miss Leslie, and certainly made her look as if no slang word could ever have passed her delicate lips.

"Is it like ? " he said, rather eagerly. " She's so difficult to do ; it's hardly possible to make her *spirituelle* enough, and I only did it from memory. Is it really like ? "

" Yes, indeed. I was with her all this afternoon, so I have her fresh in my memory. It is *very* like."

He looked at it discontentedly. " It does not do her justice," he said ; " but that's not easy. I suppose she told you how I dragged her about from place to place and stuffed her coach full of queer people, though, I dare say, she thought none of them as queer as myself," and he gave Miranda a quick upward glance from under his shaggy brows.

"She was enchanted when she heard who you were, and said she was wild about art, and that it was an honor to have had a *tête-à-tête* drive with you," said Miranda, smiling. She did not add that she had called him a nice beast; and when she saw how pleased he looked, she thought it was quite as well she had not mentioned it.

"Well now," cried he, "let's go to work and finish Miranda, at least as much of her as can be done out of the studio."

So Miranda sat to him, serene and lovely, and thinking of Mr. Gregory all the time.

CHAPTER XI.

LOVE.

THE next morning dawned fair and radiant, ushering in one of our lovely English summer days, unsurpassed in beauty by those of any other country on this globe. Did it know what it bore in its bosom for Miranda? or was it as unconscious as the child herself when she danced gayly forth to meet Mr. Gregory at Miss Hitchcock's? Never again, Miranda, will you be quite the same as you are to-day; be it joy or be it sorrow that lies before you, it is a new joy or a new sorrow; and the old life, the beautiful life of your childhood, is vanishing from you, never to be yours again—never more! No knell of departing days sounded in her ears—no chime of brighter joys fast coming. She danced on in her innocent gayety, thinking neither of the past nor of future, only of the all-sufficient present. She was to see him, and that was enough for her. But how or why the seeing him should be enough for her she never thought of asking herself.

And so she rang the bell of No. —, Eaton Place, and was ushered by the same servant into the same pretty little sitting-room where she had conversed with Mr. Hitchcock the day before. But it was not Mr. Hitchcock who joined her now; it was Lady Gregory's nephew.

A sudden, rapid memory took her back to the first moment she had ever seen him, before she had so much as heard him speak, when the tall, handsome, fashionable man had gravely offered her his arm and asked her to dance.

"You will excuse my not waiting for an introduction," he had said; "but I am Lady Gregory's nephew."

She could not tell why she thought of this first meeting, when their souls were strangers to each other, now that he came up to her with the eagerness and warmth of a friend, pressed her hand in his, and said, "You have come!"

"Yes," she replied, softly, "I have come."

"Is anyone with you?"

"No; I am quite alone. How is she to-day? is she better?"

"Yes; she is a good deal better; the doctors begin to say now that they think she will recover."

"And where is her father?"

"He has gone out of town. He could not bear to have such a case of serious illness in the house."

"No; he is a horribly selfish man."

"Now," said he, "I have something to say to you—something I have wished to say almost from the first minute in which I saw you, that minute which I shall never forget as long as I have the power of remembering anything—and I must say it now, because I am obliged to leave London.

"To leave London!" cried she, in dismay. "Oh! not really?"

"Thank you," he said, with some agitation of manner. "You may be sure I would not go unless I was forced; but thank you for caring."

"Of course I care."

"I shall not stay long—only a few days; I shall return the first possible moment; but I can't bear to go without speaking, because—because—who knows what may happen in a few days even?"

"But what is it you want to say?"

"Ay, what is it?" cried he. "What is it? Dare I tell you! Can you assure me that I dare tell you?

I have brought you here on purpose, and I stand before you powerless—the veriest coward that ever crawled upon the earth."

"You a coward! Oh, how can you say so?"

"Do you believe in love at first sight?"

"In love at first sight? Oh, dear, no, of course not; does anybody?"

"Yes—I do."

"But love must be founded on respect, on esteem, on a knowledge of character."

"Must it? Not so—not founded on them like other feelings; or whence comes it that it is *love?* How does it differ, then, from friendship, or calm, fraternal regard? No, believe me when I tell you that love—man's love for woman—comes in a moment, divining character, and itself laying the foundation for the esteem you speak of."

"Does it?" half sighed Miranda, with strange, trembling sensations creeping over her.

"It does; and then from it springs the return a woman can make—far different, much cooler—half gratitude, half gentle regard, out of which the warmer feeling will surely come. If a girl feels she has *that* for a man who would willingly *die* to possess her as his own, let her be content."

He spoke in strong, suppressed agitation. His deep voice trembled, and his dark eyes shot fire.

Miranda stood like one in a dream, her lovely face suffused with blushes, her eyes downcast, her breast softly heaving.

He could resist his own passion—he could keep back what he felt—no longer.

"I love you!" cried he.

She stretched out her hands in a sort of appeal, and seemed almost as if she would fall; but in that instant she was clasped to his heart, and held there with a tender force that she had neither the power nor the will to resist.

"He loved her! Was it possible? Was this the meaning of it all? And—she loved him! And with that thought her face was hidden on his shoulder, and she yielded herself to those protecting arms.

He felt the shy, loving movement.

"My darling—my darling—my own darling!" he cried, triumph in his voice, and passionate joy in his eyes; "you love me—you love me!"

But she drew herself away from him, and stood there, and turned her lovely eyes on him with their frank, innocent, startled gaze.

"Yes," she said, almost in a whisper, "I love you."

Then she hid her face in her two little hands, and, affrighted at her own boldness, would have run away.

But how could she run away when he was there to prevent her?

And so some minutes passed in that sweetest of all converse—the first fresh words and vows of newly spoken love.

After many and many fond expressions and tender questions, with their happy replies, he said, suddenly. "And now, my darling, only think—I don't even know your christian name."

"Miranda," replied she, shyly.

"Mi-ran-da!" said he, dwelling tenderly on the syllables. "What a sweet name, and how exactly your own. But we must change the other part of it very soon; it must not continue to be Miranda Style."

With a sudden start she withdrew herself from the arm that had again encircled her.

"Oh, I had forgotten—I had forgotten!" she cried. There was terror in her eyes and despair in her voice. "It is all over—all—all over!"

And she wrung her hands and looked at him with a grief and a remorse that he felt he never could forget. He was silent from sheer astonishment.

"I am not Miss Style, and you won't wish to—" Marry me—was the natural conclusion of the sentence, but her newly awakened heart could not say such words as those even to itself.

"You will never like me again. I am not Miss Style. I am an impostor; but I didn't meant it. Oh, I didn't mean it!" she cried.

"My darling, what are you talking about?"

"I am not Miss Style. I am an impostor. I am —a dressmaker."

"You are not Miss Style? You are a dressmaker? My dear love, are you mad? or do you think I am a fool who will believe anything that is said to him?"

"You *must* believe me," she cried, in strong agitation. "I am telling you the simple, miserable truth; but I didn't mean it—it was done all in joke. I never thought about it when I was with you, except for an instant now and then, when it seemed so amusing. I was thinking only of you, and so it never occurred to me; and I never guessed—I had not an idea that you—you *know* I had not an idea —or I would have told you at once. I never, never meant to deceive you for a moment. Oh! you must believe me when I say *that*."

"Be calm, my dearest, I will believe anything; but *what* — what, in Heaven's name, does it all mean?"

"Oh, I am not your dearest. You will never— *like* me—again. I am a dressmaker!"

"A—dress—maker!"

"Of course, I am a lady. Papa was a clergyman, but he died so poor, and Sissy did not like me to be a governess, so we work for Madam La Gai."

"Where I met you?" he cried he, still utterly bewildered.

"Yes, yes, where I met you; and I went to that ball in Miss Hitchcock's wedding dress."

He stared at her with a sort of blank look in his face, then he took hold of one of his hands in the other and pinched it violently.

"I feel the pain," said he, still staring at her. "I am not asleep. Am I going mad?"

"No, no," she cried. "Don't look at me so. You are not mad; you are only hearing just what I say. Oh! don't speak to me as you did to Maria; she was only foolish, and I was wicked; but I shall die if you speak to me as you did to her. I had just finished the dress, and I was so silly that I put it on; indeed I never did such a thing before. I can't think why I did it then, but I felt as if I couldn't help it. And then I didn't know it when I put on the dress ; but there was a ball next door, and I slipped out and slipped in and followed them up stairs. Oh, the joy of it ! Oh, how happy it was !"

And an expression of delight came suddenly into her agonized face, while she gave him a radiant smile.

And the same instant she felt herself clasped to his heart.

" My darling," he cried, " what does it matter who you are. It is yourself that I love, whatever your name may be."

The happiness of the next few minutes was something more than is often given to mortals to know. And when, at last, they came out of the blissful dream, Miranda was able to explain more coherently what had passed, and how it had all happened. She found, not that she was forgiven, but that she was not considered to have done anything that required forgiveness. Her lover, from the first, clearly understood her innocent daring, and in some way, and for some reason that she could scarcely enter into, loved her all the better for it.

When she was composed enough, she told him her own and Sophy's sad story, and how they had worked to support themselves since their father's death. In the midst of this little history her real name has been mentioned, and she spoke of Brookfield, the living that her father had been rector of, where she had been born, and where her happy childhood had glided away; but when the name passed her lips, Mr. Gregory interrupted her with vehemence.

"Brookfield!" he cried. "Maxwell! Is it possible then, my love, that you are the daughter of Mr. Maxwell of Brookfield? Why, I have heard his name all my life; he was at college with my uncle Charles, and was his intimate friend. Uncle Charles is a clergyman too."

"How wonderful!" cried Miranda. "Then after all we are old family friends. How delightfully everything always turns out!"

"Never till now—now always," replied he, tenderly. "My life was all astray till I met you— nothing went well. Now I am sure it will all be like marriage bells. And when—when—*when* will those marriage bells sound for us, Miranda?"

He addressed her by her name, for the first

time, as if a whole world of joy lay in the very sound.

"Oh!" she cried, "surely we are happy enough now without wishing for any change?"

"No," he said, boldly, "we are not—I am not. I shall never be content till you are my own."

"I am that now," she said in a whisper.

"You are not," he cried. "See, I must go out of town, and I cannot take you with me."

"Then why do you go?"

"Ah! why, indeed? Why do we let business or duties, even the most important, stand between us and the little, little happiness we can ever know?"

"*Little* happiness?"

"No, no—great, immense, overwhelming, satisfying. I speak only of time. Life is so short."

"Short!" cried she, astonished; "it seems to me like a lovely, endless valley that at last only melts into the sky."

And she sighed, and lifted up her eyes as if she *saw* heaven.

"I am not an angel like you," was his only answer.

"But why are you going out of town?" said she, smiling; "and I want you to know Sissy."

"Ah! do you remember when you refused to introduce me to her?"

"Ah yes! Do you recollect such little things? How affronted you were!"

"But the reason why I *must* go down to the Hall (my home, you know—*your* home, Miranda) is, that I have made appointments there about buying and selling land. There are lawyers and people to meet me. It has been long arranged, and this is the only time it can be done. A neighbor on whom it all depends is just of age, and must act now, as he is going abroad immediately."

"Very well, then; as soon as ever you come back I will introduce you to Sissy. How you will like her."

"And she—will she like me?"

"Like you! What a question! Of course she will."

"And then," said he, "when I come back, I must see Miss Hitchcock. She will be well enough then, I suppose, and we will finally settle that disagreeable business." His brow clouded for a moment, but when he looked at her it cleared again.

"What business have you with her, poor thing?"

"My love, have you forgotten?"

"Forgotten? No! Why, she was not deceived too, was she? She does not suppose I am Miss Style?"

"Well, yes, she does, though I don't see what that has to do with it."

"And Maria, your cousin? No, I know she does not, because they tried the mantle on me that day I sang to them, you know. Oh! but Miss Hitchcock was there too, and called me 'that young woman;' so she cannot have known who I was."

"How extremely impertinent!" said he, coloring deeply.

"No, don't mind," she said, coaxingly; "it wasn't impertinent; she thought I was there on purpose. It was all a mistake; and Madame La Gai was so sorry, and told me it should never happen again."

"I think, then, that Madame La Gai must have said something to support your dignity that misled them all; for certainly, they, one and all of them, believe you are Miss Style. I know they were extremely puzzled by your likeness to yourself at the ball, and Maria questioned her the next day, and asked if you were not really a lady, and had been at play with them; and from what she said in reply, Maria had not a doubt you were Miss Style, indeed she assured me Madame La Gai had told her so. I know Hitchcock thought so when he sent me after you yesterday."

"Then I have been going everywhere under false pretences, and I had not the least idea of it; and when they, any of them, referred to masquerading, I was in such a fright, thinking, for the moment, that they had found out about Miss Hitchcock's wedding dress."

"Yes," said he, smiling at her; "see what it is to have a guilty conscience."

"And all this time everybody has thought I was Miss Style!"

"And I am so glad you are not. I am so glad you are Miranda Maxwell."

"Are you really? And just now I thought you would give me up because I was myself. Oh, how miserable I was! I wonder whether I should have died. I do think I should; not just that minute you know, but in a little time."

There was only one reply he could make to this speech, given, as it was, so entirely from her heart. When he had made it, she said, "But why are you particularly anxious Miss Hitchcock should know who I really am?"

"My love, I am not in the least anxious. I don't care a halfpenny about it; in fact, I am not particularly anxious for anything, except that everybody should, as soon as possible, know you as my wife."

Miranda blushed beautifully at the word. .

"But," said she, rather timidly, "you said you must explain it to her, and that it would be very disagreeable."

"No, no—not *it*. I was not referring to *that*. My darling, have you really *forgotten* that I was engaged to Miss Hitchcock, and that the empty form of that engagement—it was never anything more—must be broken off? I should have done it before I spoke to you at all, but for this accident she has met with."

It was now Miranda's turn to look at him in blank amazement, only she really did not seem capable of taking in the meaning of the words.

"Engaged to Miss Hitchcock!" she repeated slowly, and like a person speaking in her sleep. "You!"

"Yes, of course, I," he said, rather impatiently. "You have known it from the first. You knew it before we met."

She put her hands to her forehead and pushed back her hair, as if she thought it oppressed her head.

"*You* engaged to Miss Hitchcock!" she said again, and still incredulously, though this time with a little fear in her voice; "but Mr. Cressingham?—surely—he—Mr. Cressingham?" and her tones rose almost shrilly (if shrillness and Miranda could be named together) as she repeated the name.

"It is not possible," he cried. "You *must* know—there *cannot* be a double misunderstanding. Why do you look so? Why do you speak so? You *must* know that *I* am Mr. Cressingham!"

"You!" cried Miranda; that was all she said.

Then there was a minute's silence. He stood, his eyes fixed upon her, astonished and uneasy; but she? he could not unravel the mystery that he found in her face. And so they stood looking at each other—these two, who, so short a space of time back, had believed that the world held nothing but happiness for them both.

"My dearest love," cried he at last, "what *is* the matter with you? What difference *does* it make?" and he laughed, or tried to laugh. "Of course I am Mr. Cressingham. I had not the slightest idea that you did not know it."

"You are Mr. Cressingham," said she. "You are engaged to Miss Hitchcock."

"Don't say it in that way," he cried, with sudden anger. "Yes, *I* am Mr. Cressingham. *I* am engaged to Miss Hitchcock. What then?"

"Then you are not engaged to me!"

"My darling, don't say so. I *am* engaged to you—doubly, trebly engaged to you—engaged by all that is dear on earth or sacred in heaven. I am *not* engaged to her. A stupid form has passed between us, nothing more; it can be blown away by a breath."

"Oh no!" said Miranda, drearily; "you are hers. You are not mine. I will not have you."

"You will not have me!"

"No; you are not good; you are not noble." She wrung her hands in agony. "You are hers; you are not mine."

"I am yours by every law, human and divine, Miranda, and I will not give you up."

"And my life rise from her death?"—she shuddered as she spoke—" the death of her happiness and her hope! Oh no, no; you have promised yourself to her, and you must have her."

"That I will *not*. I will break off the engagement; it is an unholy one. I was blind when I made it; I see now."

"And she?"

"Oh! she—she," he cried, impatiently—"she is not worthy of a thought; a hard, heartless woman to stand in *our* way—in the way of *our* love! She does not care a straw for me."

"She does," said Miranda, with the air of one who solemnly pronounced her own death-warrant; and, indeed, what else did she do when she uttered those words? "She does; I know—I feel she does. Oh yes, you must marry her; you have promised it, and it must be."

"Are you heartless too?" cried he, with sudden passion. "Oh, I see—I understand—you do not love me."

She shook her head sorrowfully.

"Oh, yes," she said, "I love you; did I not tell you so? Why should you doubt it? Love cannot change; can it? I suppose I shall love you for ever; shall I not?"

She seemed really asking him, as if for information she was anxious to have.

"Miranda," he said, in an agony of love, anger, and apprehension, "what do you mean? If you love me, what does it matter? Are you afraid that I do not really love you? I swear to you, by everything I hold dear, that I have never loved anyone else, and that my affection will only cease with my life. Then, if we both love each other, why should you care? This past folly—this mistake I have made—will soon be over; no one will be the worse for it; and you and I will be perfectly happy—you and I, Miranda."

Everything was gone from his manner, as he finished speaking, but love, and he ran up to her to take her again in his arms, but she pushed him back from her with a sort of horror.

"You are not good," she said; "I can't marry you; and you are bound to *her*."

"You told me yourself," cried he, trembling with impatience, "that an engagement might be broken off—that it was better not to make false vows. I will go to her—I will tell her—I will ask her to break it off, and she will consent. And then I will come to you, and you will receive me." There was almost defiance in his tone, as if he would force her to give an answer which he knew she was going to refuse to make.

"No," she said; "I shall not. Let me go away; I can't bear this any longer; my heart is breaking. But you are not good, and I can't marry you."

"You have no heart!" he cried. "I have poured

out all the wealth of my love on one who cannot return it."

"Let me go," she said, faintly, and moved towards the door.

He placed himself between her and it.

"Will you marry me?" he said, fiercely.

"No, I will not," said sorrowful Miranda.

"Because I am not good?"

"Yes; because you are not what I thought you, and because I cannot make that other miserable."

"That other! And have you no thought for me? Am not I miserable? And have you not even a tear for me, Miranda?"

"A tear!" cried Miranda, astonished, and touching her dry eyes with her hand. "Am I not crying? Ah, how happy I used to be when I cried! I suppose I shall never shed any more tears ever again."

There was something indescribably pathetic in the way in which she said these words; and her lover, proud, strong, indignant as he was, felt as if he could have cried himself as he heard them.

"Don't speak to me any more," she said. "Let go—it is of no use."

"Go," he said; "but if you care for me, you will

come back; if you do not, I must bear my misery as I can."

Miranda came up close to him. She touched him lightly on the shoulder with one hand, and looked earnestly in his face.

"You must marry her if she will," she said, softly, "and make her happy if you can ; and then—oh! my love, if you do this, we may meet in heaven."

CHAPTER XII.

THE END.

THERE had been some noise in the house that threatened interruption, or perhaps Mr. Cressingham might not have let Miranda go even then. She left him she scarcely knew how; and he hardly knew that she was gone till he looked round and found himself alone.

As for her, she walked home like a creature in a dream. She did not feel the pavement under her feet; she did not see the people who passed or met her. Nothing was real—nothing was alive; despair was in her heart and in her face, and her meaningless eyes looked steadily on, with a hopeless, dead look in them, which, with her white cheeks and rapid, changeless pace, drew the momentary attention of many a passenger, wrapped in his own business, towards her. One benevolent man, the father of growing-up daughters, turned and followed her a little way; but this was just as she reached home; and when he saw her enter her home, he went on his own route again with quite a sigh of relief.

She let herself in. She crept noiselessly up stairs, ashamed and afraid; and entering the little garret, which had witnessed many a day all the sweet gayety of her girlish spirits, she flung herself prostrate on the bed, and buried her poor, tearless face in the pillow.

She lay thus for many hours.

At last Sophy found her—patient Sophy, who had been working below—working, watching, and wondering—waiting for her darling to come home to her, with bright hopes in her heart of what her darling might have to say. At last she went up stairs to get some more thread, and there she found her.

The smart bonnet and Indian shawl were on the floor, and Miranda herself lay crushed together, as it were, on the bed, her pretty hair all hanging about her, her dress in disorder, and when she sat up and stared at Sophy her face was ghastly white, her eyes sunk, with black circles round them, and her fair face shocking to behold.

She began to speak instantly, before Sophy had time even to exclaim.

"Oh! Sissy," she said, "it is all over—it is all over. Oh! what shall I do?—what shall I do?"

"Miranda, you frighten me. What is the matter? Some dreadful thing has happened; what is it?"

"Some dreadful thing has happened; what is it?" repeated Miranda, in a tone of wonder. Then it all rushed back upon her. "Oh yes—I know—I know—dreadful, indeed—dreadful, indeed! He is not good, Sissy—he is not good—he is not good!"

And again she sank down, and again her face was hidden in the pillow, and her slight figure almost concealed by all the chestnut hair that lay about it.

"He has insulted you!"

"Insulted me!" cried she, sitting up again. "He loves me so he could not insult me, and I love him. Oh! what shall I do? I love him. What shall I do?—what shall I do?"

"Did he tell you he loved you?" cried Sophy, eagerly. "Did he ask you to marry him?"

"Oh yes."

"And you?"

"Did you know I loved him, Sissy? I didn't; but oh, how happy we were! How long ago is it, I wonder? It seems years. Is it really only to-day?"

"But, Miranda, my dear, what is all this about? What *has* happened?"

"He is engaged to Miss Hitchcock!"

"Who? Mr. Cressingham is—is not he?"

"No, no. Mr. Gregory is—Mr. Gregory is Mr. Cressingham, and he is engaged to Miss Hitchcock. There now, you know it all. Do you think I shall die, Sissy? Some people do die young—mamma did. Oh, how I hope I may!"

"Miranda, don't talk so—pray, don't talk so; I can't bear it, my love. But what do you mean, then? I thought you said he had offered to *you*."

"So he did."

"And that you accepted him."

"So I did."

"Then what *is* the matter, and *who* is engaged to Miss Hitchcock?"

"He is. Oh, *won't* you understand? Will nobody ever understand? Must I go always on explaining and explaining this dreadful story?"

"My darling, I don't think you know what you are saying."

"Sophy, George left you; but he was obliged to leave you, was he not? He was quite, quite good; wasn't he?"

This sudden plunge into the long-buried and never-spoken-of past—this abrupt reference to the old love story she did not know the child sister had clearly understood, took poor Sophy's breath away. A great awe seized on her; it seemed like some one speaking just before death, whose departing voice might touch any subject, however sacred.

"Yes," she answered, solemnly, after the pause of one affrighted moment; "he left me because we could not afford to marry; he was the best man I ever knew, except papa."

"Then you are happy—immensely happy, though you may never see him again. Poor Sophy—poor Sophy! you are happier than I am. *Mine* is not good!"

The words came out with a sort of wail. She pushed her face down among the pillows, as if she would fain hide it for ever, and moaned pitifully.

"Now, Miranda, my darling, you must tell me what it all means," said Sophy, soothingly, after a little time, during which she allowed her sister to give full vent to her emotions. "You must really tell me what he has done."

"As if I hadn't told you," said she, in a weary

way. "He is not Mr. Gregory. That has been my mistake all the time. He is Mr. Cressingham."

"Oh, Miranda!"

"And he is engaged to Miss Hitchcock."

"Then he has been only amusing himself with you," said Sophy, in a shocked, pained, miserable voice.

"Amusing himself!" cried Miranda, bolt upright on the bed again. "Oh, he loves me so; and I love him so; and the other was all a mistake—he doesn't care for her, or she for him, he thinks—and he means to break it off directly."

"Oh, my darling! not really? Then it is all right? Then what *is* the matter?"

"All right, Sissy, when he was engaged to her; and when she must be made unhappy; and when he has *done wrong*!—he who I thought was like an angel out of heaven. All right! And the only hope I have in the world is that my heart may really break, and that I may die. Oh, hearts do break," she added, wildly. "Don't you remember the story in the *Diary of a Physician* of the girl whose lover forsook her, and her heart broke at the piano? She went on and on, trying to be as usual, and to live it out; and she sat down to sing something, and they put his favorite song before her, and she began to sing it; and then her heart broke, and she died."

"Don't, Miranda—please don't. I really think you are making yourself miserable about nothing. I really think he has done nothing wrong that you need mind. These sort of things do happen. Men do make mistakes. I really think that you may be as happy as possible."

"Sissy!"

"I think Mr. Gregory—Mr. Cressingham, I mean —may be a very good man—a very good man indeed; though he did make a mistake when he was quite young, and engage himself to Miss Hitchcock."

"Oh! would papa think so?"

Sophy reflected a moment, then she sent up a little prayer for guidance, and then she kissed Miranda's white face, and said, solemnly—

"Yes, my darling, I believe he would."

Miranda sat motionless, as if she had fallen into a trance—motionless, speechless, amazed. After a while she began to tremble, and then she began to weep. Her tears seemed endless—they poured forth out of her eyes, big, bright, and beneficent—endless, as if she had never shed any before in her life, and was never to shed any again.

At last she spoke.

"Then I can bear anything else," she said. "Of course I must not think of him, except as a friend; but I was very happy in his friendship before I knew better, and I must try to be content now."

"But why should you not marry him when he has broken off the engagement?"

"Oh, don't, Sissy, don't!" she said, shrinking; "you hurt me. First, it is so wrong to *think* of such a thing while he is still engaged; and then, *if* she was made unhappy, I never could—no, I never could —I should be haunted by her all my life."

And Miranda thought, with a shudder, of a bride in the looking-glass—Miss Hitchcock in her wedding dress — whom she had fancied, during the weary watch she had kept by her bedside, was shut up there to haunt her for ever. She had made that ghost vanish by walking boldly forward and looking for it. "Are these strong, senseless impressions always allegories, symbols, prophecies?" thought she, with vague superstition, "Is it the thought of the real bride that was to be, that is to haunt my life if I take her place? and is it only by straight-forward courage that I can lay her ghost? Was that haunting fancy at once a prevision of our future life, and a lesson how to avoid it? Was it for that, that circumstances led me in so unexpected a manner to watch by a stranger's bedside?"

It was getting late, and Sophy now begged Miranda to undress and go to bed to try and get some sleep.

"Yes, I will give in this one night, because I really couldn't sit up," Miranda confessed; "but after that I must be as usual. I may have a long time to wait; I may have to wait all my life. He may marry her, or he may not be able to break off the engagement soon, or she may be made unhappy; and all that while I must not even *think* of him— not in my own heart—not even in my prayers—except as a friend; and so I must begin at once, to-morrow, and work, and talk, and be just as usual, or else I shall be cheating and not *really* doing it; but just now I will not try to be strong, because I *am* so weak; so I will undress, as you tell me, and go to bed, and perhaps by-and-by I may get a little, *little* sleep."

Some sleep Miranda did get, but in the middle of the night she woke Sophy.

"Sissy," she said, "I am so *very* sorry I was so selfish—I thought only of myself, and not one bit of you; and I didn't know it—I hadn't an idea of it. That's the worst of being selfish; one is horrid, and one doesn't know it. I was just like Mr. Hitchcock."

"But what did you do, dear? I don't know of anything. You were very unhappy, poor child; that was all."

"I talked of breaking my heart and dying young," said Miranda, indignantly; "as if I could *think* of such a thing, however much I might wish it, when there's you! I ought to have been ashamed of myself, that I ought, and so I am. Me to die young, indeed, and leave my poor old Sophy—that *would* be a pretty thing to do."

And she crept up to Sophy's side and fondled her, and went to sleep with her head on her breast.

After that night Miranda kept her word. She went about her work as usual, and was as brave and as strong as a good girl could be. She might not laugh quite as often, or chat quite as gayly as her wont, and her cheeks might have lost a little of their delicate wild-rose tint, but that was all; in sweetness, goodness, industry, and even cheerfulness, she was Miranda still.

She knew that Mr. Cressingham was out of

town—that there was no fear of her meeting him; yet she did not go near either Miss Hitchcock or Maria Leslie. It was under a mistake that they had known her. To them she was Miss Style. She knew not how to undeceive them; but she would not associate with them except as herself, and as herself she supposed they would not care to have her. To Miss Hitchcock, of course, under no circumstances would she go; and *she* must still be too ill to want anybody, or to think about her at all. But perhaps Maria might wonder why she did not walk in some afternoon, to four o'clock tea, to sing *Far Away*, "perfectly in tune," to the excruciating sounds of the creaky, creaky organ. How like a dream that song now seemed, at the end of which *he* had pushed open the door and entered the room! Was she really the same girl who stood there singing, and been left alone with him when Maria had run, crying, away from them? But here she found herself on dangerous ground, and her thoughts had to be reined in and turned forcibly in an another direction—a thwarting which always happened to them when they got upon dangerous ground, which they perhaps did something about forty times in every hour; but no one could be more conscientious or determined than Miranda was in always turning them off it again.

It was just about this time that Mr. Gaunt entreated her to pay him the long-promised visit to his studio and give him one final sitting for his portrait of Miranda. She agreed to do this. Sophy accompanied her, and they spent a pleasant half-hour looking over his pictures.

"If your friend, Miss what's-her-name, is so wild about Art," said he, suddenly, in his gruffest tones, "why doesn't she come and have a look at him here?"

"I dare say because you didn't ask her," replied Miranda, smiling.

"And how could I ask her when I didn't know she cared twopence-ha'penny about it?" cried he, angrily. "Why don't you tell her she may come?"

"I never see her now," said Miranda, with a half sigh.

"Oh, a fickle, fashionable friend! Yes, yes, I see," sneered Mr. Gaunt.

"No, you don't," answered she. "She may be fashionable—I'm sure I don't know whether she is or not—but she is not fickle; it is I have not been to see her; I have been busy—and—I did not go."

"Well, there you are complete as Miranda, at any rate," cried he, flinging down his brush ; "and you may walk miles and miles before you see a prettier picture—hang it all !"

The two sisters paid their tribute of praise to the picture, warm and honest enough to satisfy even the artist ; after which they strolled home together, talking softly as they went of all they had seen.

When they entered the little back parlor, Miranda sank listlessly into a chair.

"Oh, I am so tired," she said.

"What's that?" said Sophy, her eye falling on a few inches of white that lay on the table.

Miranda turned languidly and took it up.

"A note!" she cried, surprised; adding, "for me," with some emotion.

Then she opened and read it, and looked up at her sister with a meek, defenceless look.

"Oh, Sissy, what can this mean?"

And then she read aloud—

"'Miss Hitchcock presents her compliments to Miss Miranda Maxwell, and will be much obliged if she can call on her this afternoon, between five and six o'clock.'"

"Oh, Sissy, what shall I do?"

"Well, my dear, I think you must go."

"To her? Of all the people in the world—to her!"

"You have behaved nobly by her. You have done all that was right. You need not be the least afraid to see her. Why should you not go?"

"Oh, I don't know."

"Probably it is only to thank you for having nursed her; or perhaps about some millinery business. You were at her house, you know, on some such errand when she met with the accident."

"He has told her my name! She knows I am not Miss Style!"

"My dear, do you wish *not* to go?"

"I don't know. I believe I wish I had not got this note; but since I *have* got it, I could not bear to keep away."

"Then take my advice and go at once, without thinking any more about it; it is past five o'clock now."

"Oh yes, it is so easy to *say* that—to go without thinking about it," murmured Miranda, as she arranged her bonnet at the glass; and then she kissed Sophy, and—went.

She hardly knew whether she thought at all, as she walked from her own house to Miss Hitchcock's. But when she rang the bell at the end of her journey, her cheeks were hot, her hands cold and her heart beat fast.

The door was opened to her by the smart page, who smiled his recognition, and then handed her over to the same maid who had declined making herself useful when her mistress had met with an accident, because it was not down in any of her characters. She conducted her to the drawing-room floor—how familiar it all seemed to Miranda, and yet how strange—and, opening a door there, ushered her into a dressing-room, or boudoir, luxuriously furnished and full of flowers. There on a sofa lay Miss Hitchcock, browner, plainer, and more disagreeable-looking than ever, and dressed by the dictates of her evil genius in a white peignori covered with embroidery and trimmed with delicate mauve ribbons. Why was that poor woman always forced to put on things the prettiest in themselves, yet the most unbecoming to her unfortunate person? That is a hard fate which, nevertheless, attends some people through life. Is it by something incongruous—something that jars in their own minds that they deserve it? Is it a sort of poetical justice understood by nobody, and least of all by themselves? Miranda stood timidly by the door, looking at the ugly woman in her beautiful room, and charming, unbecoming invalid dress—looking at her, but not daring to approach her.

"What has he told her about me?—what has he told her about me?" was the one thought in her mind.

"Is that you, Miss Maxwell?" said the pleasant voice she remembered so well, and which now sent a little thrill all over her; "pray, come here—pray, do not stand by the door."

Miranda advanced towards the lady like a puppet moved by strings. She tried to speak, but her tongue seemed parched, and could not utter a word. Then Miss Hitchcock laughed her peculiarly disagreeable, harsh laugh.

"Are you afraid of me?" said she.

Miranda asked herself the question, "Am I?" She raised her eyes frankly to meet the forbidding eyes fixed on her, and answered, "No, I am not afraid of you—there is no reason why I should be."

"Scarcely," said the other. "I want to thank you for watching by me when no one else would; the doctor thinks you saved my life."

This was quite a new idea to Miranda. The color rushed into her cheeks that had been pale with suppressed emotion, and joy danced in her eyes.

"Did I really?" she cried.

There was no mistaking what she felt.

"You are glad?" said Miss Hitchcock, pleasantly, regarding her at the same time with a stern, almost spiteful countenance.

"Glad?" cried Miranda. "I should think so!"

"You are a good girl."

"Good, because I am glad I saved your life?" and she laughed a little.

"Yes, if that life came in the way of your own happiness."

"As if that would make any difference!"

"No difference in the act perhaps, but in the joy that follows the act."

"Besides," said Miranda, blushing brightly, and speaking very timidly indeed, "it could not come in the way of any happiness which belongs to it, and to no one else."

"Ah!" said Miss Hitchcock, "people don't always think of whether a thing is their own, if they can anyhow get it."

Miranda was silent for a minute, and then said, "Are you much better? Are you getting quite well?"

"Yes," replied the other; "I am much better; I am getting quite well; I shall soon be well enough to be married. Have you got my wedding dress safe?"

Miranda was covered with blushes, and had not a word to say for herself. She felt dreadfully ashamed.

"It fitted you exactly, did it not? Do you think it will fit me as well? Do you know I have never tried it on?"

"Pray, forgive me," said Miranda, gently. "I am so very sorry."

"Sorry—dear me! forgive you—what for? What have you done?"

"For wearing your wedding dress," said she at once, frankly and timidly. "It was very wrong of me. I am glad you know of it, so that I can ask your pardon."

"And is that the greatest injury you have done me?" said the other.

Miranda reflected.

"Yes," she said. "I have done you no other injury that I could help."

"Will you come to my wedding?" said Miss Hitchcock, abruptly.

"No," replied Miranda, in great haste; "I will not."

"Shall I come to yours?"

Miranda was silent.

"Will you wear my wedding dress?"

She looked up like a startled fawn.

"You have surely some meaning in what you are saying?"

"Do you think people ever pass through a great danger conscious of that danger, and come out of it just the same as they went into it?"

"No," replied Miranda, thoughtfully; "I don't suppose they ever do."

"I had plenty of time for reflection when I was ill," continued Miss Hitchcock; "and I saw a good many things in new lights; and I made a great many plans for the future, if any future was to be mine. But nothing came so vividly before me as the fact that Arthur Cressingham and Hannah Hitchcock made a great mistake when they promised to marry each other."

Miranda pressed her hand against her heart to still its rapid beating.

"And so the first thing I did when I got better was to send for him and tell him so, and give him back his promise and ask for mine."

Miranda grew paler and paler, and pressed her hand harder against her little trembling, fluttering heart.

"You did!"

"I did; and he quite agreed with me."

"And it was you who did it first!" cried Miranda. "And you didn't know of me! Thank God—thank God."

"My dear child, are you about to faint? Pray don't; I'm not strong enough to help you."

"This is going too far," said Mr. Cressingham, advancing suddenly from Miranda had not the slightest idea where, and catching her in his arms just as she would have fallen to the ground.

But she rapidly came to herself again. The spirit was too happy not to be eager to return to the form that was encircled by those dear arms. Almost the first thing she said was, in the softest whisper, "Forgive me; I blamed you too much; I did not understand—" He stopped the words with kisses, and assured her that he had deserved every word she said. And so all Miranda's scruples were satisfied, and the happiness which her sweet nature was so well fitted to enjoy surrounded her like a flood of sunshine.

It is a pity to draw stories out to any length after the denouement has occurred, and either perfect joy or perfect misery has set in. The intelligent reader —and none, we believe, but an intelligent reader will have accompanied us so far in our narrative, does not require to be told that Mr. Cressingham persuaded Miranda to fix an early day for their marriage, and that, long after that glorious day was among the has-beens of life, he continued to be the happiest of men as she was of women; for if his love had been sudden, it was deep and true; and he was one of those fortunate beings who, falling in love with an idea (for such love at first sight must always be), finds the reality surpasses instead of falling short of it.

We will, therefore, only add, what even the most intelligent reader might not divine for himself, that Mr. Cressingham, having a most excellent living in his gift, close to the Hall, managed to get rid of its rector without poisoning or otherwise maltreating him, and immediately afterwards presented it to faithful George, who, in consequence thereof, gave up his chaplaincy in India, returned home in the highest spirits, and married faithful Sophy ; and that Maria Leslie and Mr. Gaunt met very often in the course of the next year or two, but that I am not going to give the least hint as to whether anything came of it. Be that as it may, however, one thing is certain, neither Mr. Cressingham nor Miranda Maxwell ever for a moment regretted, or had any cause to regret, through the whole of their future lives, the evening when she first put on MISS HITCHCOCK'S WEDDING DRESS.

DR. HOLLAND'S
LATEST PROSE WORK,

SEVENOAKS.
A STORY OF TO-DAY.
BY J. G. HOLLAND.

Author of "ARTHUR BONNICASTLE," "THE MISTRESS OF THE MANSE,"
"KATHRINA," "BITTER SWEET," "TITCOMB'S LETTERS," etc.

With 12 full-page illustrations, after original designs by Sol. Eytinge.
One volume, 12mo. Cloth, $1.75.

Dr. Holland in his latest novel, "The Story of Sevenoaks," has undertaken to present some typical American characters, and especially to throw light upon a phase of New York life, the outside of which, at least, is familiar to every reader. Jim Fenton, the rough, droll, outspoken, big-hearted fellow, who rises from trapper to hotel-keeper in the Northern woods; Paul Benedict, the gentle, easily swindled inventor; Miss Butterworth, the brusque, busy, and benevolent little dressmaker; Mr. Snow, the conciliatory parson; Mr. Cavendish, the lawyer for an emergency; Mrs. Dillingham, the handsome semi-adventuress; Mrs. Belcher, the fretful, but too meek wife; and Belcher himself, the cunning and successful swindler, the great manufacturer, the railroad prince, the man who gets up a corner in Wall Street, and "pines for a theological seminary,"—all these, and other characters whose names we need not rehearse, each suggests some real person whom the reader has known or read about. But it is not merely because the characters and scenes and incidents are thoroughly modern and familiar that the story has won so much attention during its serial publication in SCRIBNER'S MONTHLY. The progress of events is rapid, and graphically narrated: and it is seldom that an American Magazine story has been followed from beginning to end by so large an audience, and with such eager and sustained interest. The book, too, is enlivened by those bits of out-of-door description, sympathetic touches of character, and genial philosophies, that his readers always find in Dr. Holland's stories, and which constitute no small part of their attraction.

Copies sent post-paid by

SCRIBNER, ARMSTRONG, & CO.
743 and 745 BROADWAY, NEW YORK.

POPULAR NEW BOOKS:

IMPRESSIONS OF
LONDON SOCIAL LIFE,
By E. S. NADAL. One vol. 12mo, cloth. $1.50.

During a residence of a year or two in England, as a secretary of the United States Legation, Mr. Nadal enjoyed unusual facilities for observing the inner social life of the people. He has here sketched their characteristics with the most attractive freshness and freedom, while a subtile, philosophic irony, and a delicate but keen humor, lend additional charms to a terse and elegant style. The volume is both interesting for the insight which it gives into English life, and of real value as worthily supplementing the well-known works of Emerson and Hawthorne, which discuss the same subject.

A COMPANION VOLUME TO "ROUNDABOUT RAMBLES."
TALES OUT OF SCHOOL,
By FRANK R. STOCKTON, author of "Roundabout Rambles," etc. One vol. quarto, cloth, nearly 300 illustrations, $2.50.

Few writers for the young combine the happy faculty, possessed in so remarkable a degree by Mr. Stockton, of amusing while he instructs his readers. Short stories, graphic descriptions of the strange, wonderful, and odd in nature and art, all most pleasantly rehearsed, make up a volume quite as attractive as its predecessor—*Roundabout Rambles*. The illustrations—about three hundred in all—are a striking feature of this handsome volume.

A POEM BY A NEW AUTHOR:
THE NEW DAY:
A POEM IN SONGS AND SONNETS.
By RICHARD WATSON GILDER. One vol. 12mo, with unique illustrations, especially engraved for the work by Henry Marsh. Tastefully bound in a new and beautiful style. Price $1.50.

The author has already gained reputation as assistant editor of *Scribner's Monthly* since its commencement, and by the delicate quality of "The Old Cabinet," his special department of that magazine. In literary circles he is known to be a true singer, who has bided his time before addressing his voice to a large audience. Mr. Gilder's verse is marked by an earnestness unusual in these times, and is full of subtle passion, expressed with melodious and finished art. The book will be decorated with new and beautiful designs, engraved by Henry Marsh.

For sale by all booksellers. Sent postpaid, on receipt of price, by the Publishers,

SCRIBNER, ARMSTRONG & CO.,
743 and 745 Broadway, N. Y.

"Infinite riches in a little room." —MARLOWE.

COMPLETION OF THE FIRST

BRIC-A-BRAC SERIES.

Personal Reminiscences of Famous Poets and Novelists, Wits and Humorists, Artists, Actors, Musicians, and the like.

EDITED BY

RICHARD HENRY STODDARD.

Complete in ten volumes, square 12mo. Per vol. $1.50.

The BRIC-A-BRAC SERIES has achieved for itself a success altogether exceptional in the history of publishing in this country.

OVER SIXTY THOUSAND VOLUMES

Of the first series have been sold in eighteen months. The BRIC-A-BRAC SERIES constitutes a

COMPLETE REPOSITORY OF REMINISCENCES

Of prominent men and women of this and the last century. Characteristic anecdotes of every individual of note in art, literature, the drama, politics, or society are related, and they are told by those who know how to give point to a good story.

THE SERIES COMPRISES THE FOLLOWING TEN VOLUMES:

I. CHORLEY, PLANCHÉ, and YOUNG.
II. THACKERAY and DICKENS, with fac-simile of a letter by Thackeray.
III. MÉRIMÉE, LAMARTINE, and SAND.
IV. BARHAM, HARNESS, and HODDER.
V. THE GREVILLE MEMOIRS, with Portrait of Greville.
VI. MOORE and JERDAN, with 4 Illustrations.
VII. CORNELIA KNIGHT and THOMAS RAIKES, with 4 Illustrations.
VIII. O'KEEFFE, KELLY, and TAYLOR, with 4 Illustrations.
IX. LAMB, HAZLITT, and Others, with 4 Illustrations and fac-simile of a letter by Lamb.
X. CONSTABLE and GILLIES, with 4 Illustrations.

A sixteen-page Descriptive Catalogue of the Series, containing Specimen Illustrations, sent to any address upon application.

NOW READY:

COMPLETE SETS OF THE BRIC-A-BRAC SERIES IN THE FOLLOWING STYLES:—

1. CLOTH, IN A NEAT BOX $15.00
2. HALF VELLUM, RED EDGES, in a handsome box, of an entirely new style... 17.50
3. HALF CALF, EXTRA, in a handsome box, of an entirely new style.... 20.00

Sent, post-paid, or express charges paid, on receipt of price by the Publishers,

SCRIBNER, ARMSTRONG, & CO.
743 & 745 Broadway, New York.

POPULAR AND STANDARD BOOKS
PUBLISHED BY
SCRIBNER, ARMSTRONG & CO.,
743 and 745 Broadway, New York,
In 1875.

ANCIENT HISTORY FROM THE MONUMENTS. 3 vols. 12mo, *illus.* Per vol. $1 00
  I Egypt; from Earliest Times to B.C. 300. By S. BIRCH, LL.D.
  II. Assyria; from Earliest Times to Fall of Nineveh. By GEORGE SMITH.
  III. Persia; from Earliest Period to Arab Conquest. By W. VAUX, M.A.
ALEXANDER, J. A, LIFE OF. By H. C. ALEXANDER. *New ed. at reduced price.* Two vols. in one. *Portraits.* 8vo... 2 50
BIBLE COMMENTARY. Vol. V. Isaiah, Jeremiah, and Lamentations.......... 5 00
BRIC-A-BRAC SERIES. Edited by R. H. STODDARD. 12mo, cloth. Per vol.... 1 50
  In sets of 10 volumes, half calf, $20; half vellum, $17.50; cloth.................15 00
  Moore and Jerdan. 1 vol. *With 4 illus.*
  Knight and Raikes. 1 vol. *With 4 illus.*
  O'Keefe, Kelly, and Taylor. 1 vol. *With 4 illus.*
  Lamb, Hazlitt, and others. 1 vol. *With 4 illus., and fac-simile of letter by Lamb.*
  Constable and Gillies. 1 vol. *With 4 illus.*
CRAIK, G. L. A Compendious History of English Literature. *New and cheaper ed.* 2 vols. 8vo, cloth... 5 00
DODGE, Mrs. M. M Rhymes and Jingles. *With 150 illus. New and cheaper ed* 1 50
—— Hans Brinker; or, the Silver Skates. By Mrs. M. M. DODGE. *New and elegant ed.* Crown 8vo, full gilt, $3.50; plain................................. 3 00
EUSTIS, T. W. The Service of Praise. Square crown 8vo................. 1 50
EWBANK, T. Hydraulics. 15TH EDITION. *Illus.*........................ 6 00
GILDER, R. W. The New Day: A Poem in Songs and Sonnets. 12mo..... 1 50
HARLAND, MARION. Breakfast, Luncheon, and Tea. 12mo............. 1 75
HEADLEY, J. T. Sacred Mountains, Scenes, and Characters *Illus* (*New ed.*) 12mo... 2 00
—— The Adirondack. *Illus.* (*New ed.*) 12mo.......................... 2 00
—— Washington and His Generals. 16 *Portraits.* (*New ed.*) 12mo...... 2 50
HODGE, CHARLES, LL.D. Systematic Theology. 3 vols. 8vo. *New and cheaper ed*...12 00
HOLLAND, J. G. Sevenoaks; A Story of To-Day. 12 *illus.* 12mo........ 1 75
MORRIS, W. O'C. The French Revolution and First Empire. (*In the "Epochs of History" Series.*) 3 maps. 12mo... 1 00
MÜLLER, Prof. F. MAX. Chips from a German Workshop. Vol. IV. Crown 8vo... 2 50
NADAL, E. S. Impressions of London Social Life. 12mo................ 1 50
ROUSSELET, L. India and its Native Princes. 317 *illus., many of them full-page.* Imp. 4to, cloth..25 00
SHIELDS, C.W. Religion and Science in their Relations to Philosophy. 12mo. 1 00
SMITH, GEORGE. The Chaldean Account of Genesis. By GEORGE SMITH,. 4 00
STEPHEN, L. Hours in a Library. 12mo............................. 1 75
STOCKTON, F. R. Roundabout Rambles. 200 *illus.* 4to. (*New ed.*)...... 2 00
—— Tales Out of School. *With more than 150 illus.* 4to.................. 2 50
THOLUCK, A. Hours of Christian Devotion. 12mo..................... 3 00
VERNE, J. The Mysterious Island. In Three Parts, each one vol. 12mo, cloth. *Illus.* Price, per part.. 2 00
  I. Dropped from the Clouds. 49 *full-page illus.* II. Abandoned. 49 *full-page illus.* III. The Secret of the Island. 49 *full-page illus.*

Any, or all, of the above sent, post or express charges paid, on receipt of the price, by the publishers.

www.ingramcontent.com/pod-product-compliance
Lightning Source LLC
Chambersburg PA
CBHW032143230426
43672CB00011B/2438